Protecting Your Greatest Investment
Investing in the Needs of Children

Copyright © 2020 by Ashley S Jefferies

All rights reserved. No part of this book may be reproduced or used in any manner without written permission of the copyright owner except for the use of quotations in a book review.

ISBN 978-1-7361544-0-3 (paperback)
ISBN 978-1-7361544-1-0 (e-book)

This book is dedicated to all the
children and families
I have had the pleasure of
serving throughout my career,
CJ, who inspires me to be a better mom
And
My parents for all of their love and support
from here and above.

CONTENTS

INTRODUCTION: What am I Investing in and Why?   9

CHAPTER 1: Your Greatest Investment   17

CHAPTER 2: Investing in Physical Health: Nutrition and Exercise   29

CHAPTER 3: Investing in Emotional Health: Part 1 How do you parent?   51

CHAPTER 4: Investing in Emotional Health: Part 2 Hidden Needs   85

CHAPTER 5: Investing in Educational Health: Mindsets, Goals, and Education   117

CHAPTER 6: Investing in Relational Health: Navigating Relationships   131

CHAPTER 7: Investing in Financial Health: Money Matters   143

CHAPTER 8: Investing in Spiritual Health: Finding Their Way   161

CHAPTER 9: Conclusion: Final Thoughts   177

FOOT NOTES   185

Introduction: What Am I Investing in and Why?

The birth of a child is often a joyous occasion for moms and dads, especially when it is the firstborn child. For some parents, it is a time of celebration and hope as a new life full of possibilities is born. For other parents, it is a time of uncertainty as a new life full of the unknown has arrived into the world. Intermixed with the feeling of joy and uncertainty can be the feelings of nervousness, fear, anxiety as parents begin to realize the fate of their tiny bundle of joy lies in their hands. Most parents want the best for their children and vow to do what it takes to ensure their children have the best opportunities life has to offer. And though children do not come with instruction manuals on how to properly rear them, there are numerous reading materials, parenting classes, videos, and seminars available for parents to assistance them on their journey through parenthood.

What we leave behind to our children when we depart this earth is often more important than the possessions we collect while we are here on earth. Most people do not remember the possessions one gathered during their tenure on earth. What most people remember is what a person left behind (or did not leave behind). Old family recipes, an old car, memories, jewelry, and old sayings are just some of the things people remember when a loved one has left this earth. In other words, a person's legacy is what is remembered. The same is true for our children. They will remember the lessons and values we have poured into them more so than our material possessions.

Legacy is defined as "anything handed down from the past, as from an ancestor or predecessor." In order to leave a legacy, we must first have something to leave behind. Sadly, sometimes the only things we have to leave our loved ones is debt and heartache. What we leave behind does not always have to be tangible. Some of our most valuable possessions are not material at all. Life lessons, sage advice, old proverbs and sayings, a way of thinking, and a way of life are some examples of the intangibles we can leave behind for future generations to aid them in their journey through life. In the world we live in today, it is easy to become preoccupied with living for now. Let's face it. Some of us do not have the time, money, energy, or effort to concentrate on the future, let alone invest for our future or leave a legacy. We postpone legacy building and investing in our future today until tomorrow. However, our tomorrow has slowly become our today.

My father died when I was in my early twenties. By society standards, he was not a rich man. He was an average hard-working man who did who it took to provide for his family. When he died, he left my mom a small insurance policy, a little more than enough to cover his funeral expenses. Although he was not in the financial position to leave us with much money, the life lessons and wisdom he left behind were invaluable. He demonstrated to my sister and I what a loving father, devoted husband, good friend, dependable brother, hard worker, and wonderful son looked like. He provided a stable home environment, talked to us about finances, showed us how to have fun, and taught us how to play cards. No amount of money he could have left behind is equal to the impression he left on our lives. That was his legacy. That is what he left to us in his short 56 years on this earth.

As parents, we have been tasked with the responsibility to provide for and take care of children. We have been tasked with making sure they receive guidance and upbringing necessary to be well-adjusted and productive members of society. The time, effort, money, patience, and love we invest in our children is not for nothing. As parents, we hope that the children we have invested in grow up to make us proud! Being proud of our children, regardless of their successes and failures, is the return on the investment we make in them. When we really look at it, our children should be the greatest investment of our time, effort, knowledge, and money. The nurture, care, and love we provide our children from the time they are one hour old to the time they are grown with their own families is the investment we make in them, hoping that one day we will realize that all our time, effort, and money has not be for naught and yields an overall good, moral, decent, well-adjusted individual (our return). Therefore, it is imperative as parents we have the tools to adequate invest in our children so that the return on our investment is great.

In today's hectic society, people are busy checking the stock market and their investment portfolios, keeping an eye on their money and their investments. At the time of this writing, the stock market is doing well and the housing market has successfully rebounded from the housing crash of 2008. Unemployment rates are low and a new tax bill has just been signed, which is supposed to reduce taxes for the middle class. Economically, America is doing well.

However, when we examine the state of our educational system, criminal justice system, the family unit, poverty rates, mental health crisis rates, and rate of obesity and other health related conditions, America receives unsatisfactory or failing grades. Children are continuing to graduate high school without the ability to read or write or the knowledge and skills to compete competitively with other countries in areas such as math and science. Youth are being incarcerated at alarming rates without adequately being rehabilitated to change their actions and behaviors. The family unit is being attacked with more and more mothers and fathers being absent in their children's lives, causing grandparents and great grandparents to rear their grandchildren and great grandchildren. Crime and poverty are rampant throughout many cities and neighborhoods in America. Mass shootings and killings of

Americans by other Americans is on the rise. America, as a whole, is fatter, unhealthier society that what it was fifty, even thirty years ago.

Today's children are suffering from the decisions and the lack of investment and provisions made by past generations for the next generation. Somehow, society has dropped the ball on investing in our children. All children are not doomed, but many are suffering due to the lack of investment parents, adults, and authority figures have made in their lives. Nonetheless, it is never too late to change and shift the paradigm of America to focus more on our children's overall wellbeing. Not just simply meeting their physical needs of food, clothing, and shelter, but meeting their other needs such as socioemotional wellbeing, educational needs and investing in their sense of morality, altruism, and justice.

This book is designed to help parents, teachers, counselors, youth pastors, coaches and others who work with children and youth understand the intricacies that make up children who eventually grow into adults. It is designed to equip parents with knowledge on how to invest in their children so they are able to rear children who can function in and contribute productively to society. This is NOT a book on parenting. This book is not designed to shame parents who may not be practicing some of the principles outlined in the book. This book is NOT intended to be the end all, be all book on children. Written from the perspective of a parent and educator, it is simply designed to be a resource for parents and others who work with children to guide them as they teach their children and provide practical ideas to help adults engage more with children. I want you to keep an open mind as you read through this book. Take notes and highlight when necessary. But most of all, I want you to apply what you learn so that you can better protect your greatest investment, your children.

Chapter 1: Your Greatest Investment

Let me start by saying I am not well versed in the language of investing. I understand the basic principle of "buy low and sell high." Because of the ebb and flow nature of investing, there are periods of highs and lows. How well one is able to navigate the fluctuation determines how much return one will see on his/her investment. I also realize there are long-term versus short- term investments. With long term investments, one must ride the waves of the ups and downs in the stock market and not panic or quit when the stocks are down. Short term investments are beneficial when you are wanting to make money quickly and do not want to wait, but they are highly volatile due to the nature of the stock market. Lastly, I comprehend there are inherent risks in almost any type of investing. Beyond this, I rely on the expertise of my financial advisor when it comes to making decisions about my investments.

The concept I want you to focus on is long-term versus short term investing. Long term investments require patience and perseverance if you want the greatest return on your investments. If we adopt the idea of our children being our greatest long-term investment, then we must rear them in a way reflective of what we want our return on investment to look like. In investing, chasing a "hot tip" may not always prove to be the safest, most reliable method of investing. Picking a particular investment strategy and sticking with that strategy has proven to be more beneficial than chasing after the latest and greatest stock tip to gain the greatest gains on your investment. Although you may gain short-term success, "hot tips" are often short-lived with little gains achieved. Similarly, in rearing children, chasing the latest and greatest parenting fads versus sticking with proven parenting techniques can yield short-term success that is, however, not sustainable in the long run.

Many parents, including myself, have fallen prey to gimmicks and quick fixes that promise your child will act a certain way, be better or faster at a certain skill, or change unwanted behaviors. When I was completing research for this book, I came across some very interesting parenting fads that have come and gone. One of the more bizarre parenting fads occurred in the 1930s with the introduction of baby window cages. If you are not familiar with what a baby window cage is, you are not alone. I was not aware of it either. The baby window cage was developed as a means for babies, who lived in apartments or other buildings with decreased green space to play and run around, to get vitamin D naturally from the sun. It was further used as a means of "airing" the baby, a concept developed by Dr. Luther Emmett Holt who wrote about it in his 1894 book *The Care and Feeding of Children*.

The concept of airing was to promote health in children by increasing their exposure to fresh air. According to Dr. Holt, "Fresh air is required to renew and purify the blood, and this is just as necessary for health and growth as proper food. The appetite is improved, the digestion is better, the cheeks become red, and all signs of health are seen." With the concept of "airing," babies are exposed to cold temperatures inside and outside the home. The reasoning behind cold air exposure was to decrease a baby's chance of catching the common cold by exposing him to cold air. Therefore, parents were encouraged to bath their children in 50-60 degree water, expose them to cold temperatures via sleeping in baby window cages, cribs, or carriers hung out a window, and/or keep a cool room temperature. The concept of the baby window cage was to suspend a wire cage out of a window (instead of a crib or baby carrier) and place the baby in it in order for the little one to get some sun and fresh air. Sounds crazy, right? Well, apparently, it was a popular trend in those days and many parents opted to purchase this device. Fortunately, this trend did not last as it had faded by the middle of the 20th century.

 A second parenting fad was the idea of rubbing whiskey, yes alcohol, on an infant's gums to help with teething and the pain associated with emerging teeth. The idea was to numb the gums using alcohol to decrease toothache pain. Rubbing whiskey or other types of liquor on an infant's gums to relieve teething pain was a common remedy in the past. Fortunately, with the advancements in medicine and technology, there are safer ways to relieve toothache pain such as using teething rings or a frozen wash cloth. There is research to show there are negative, even fatal, side effects present when a baby is exposed to any amount of alcohol. Although there are still parents today who still use alcohol as a means to sooth aching gums, most pediatricians would agree there are better and safer alternatives.

For me, it was potty training. When I was trying to potty train my two-year old son, it was not an easy task. Any parent who has been through the potty-training phase knows it can be a difficult time for the parent and the child, especially for boys. I asked different parents who had successfully potty trained their children to see what they did. I was looking for the quick fix to potty training. I was instructed to let my son run around naked and take him to the potty every 30 minutes, buy his favorite character themed potty seat so that he likes to sit on the potty, and let him stay in a wet or dirty diaper so that it becomes uncomfortable to him and then he will want to use the potty.

I was skeptical about having him run around naked for fear I would find wet spots and brown bananas all over my house, so I did not do that. I did not feel right leaving him in a wet or soiled diaper just so he could learn how uncomfortable that felt. I did buy his favorite potty seat character, Mickey Mouse, which made noises. None of those quick fixes worked and I soon realized I had to simply put in the time and effort to potty train him. That meant taking him to potty after meals and keeping him on the potty until he went, talking with him about the potty experience, and letting him become comfortable with the potty on his own time. I could not rush the experience for my sake. I had to put in the time and it paid off in the end. Once he was fully potty trained, he did not have any accidents. The bottom line is there are no quick fixes and we must weigh the long-term effects on certain parenting practices before we decide a new trend is appropriate for our children.

Secondly, long-term investing requires a long-term perspective with a focus on the future. Generally, long-term perspectives have a minimum of 10 years with some long-term perspectives reaching 25 years in advance. A long-term perspective requires you to think about the future in your present circumstance, to think from the future reflecting back to the present, and/or to think about the whole picture (past, present, and future) as an overview. The perspective one takes determines the steps and actions he will pursue to achieve the expected outcomes. You must think ahead, anticipating possible changes or deviations from the planned route. When you can anticipate future challenges by reviewing different scenarios, you can better prepare for these challenges and avoid being blindsided by unexpected circumstances by adopting strategies and plans early on to combat challenges. Although we do not know the future, we can influence the future by our present actions.[1]

This long-term concept of preparing for the future can be applied to rearing children. Viewing children as our greatest investments requires parents to plan for the future now. Whether it is starting a college fund for them as soon as they are born, enrolling them in sports programs early, or enforcing disciplinary rules and consequences during the early years of life, these acts should be initiated early in life and with a proposed return on your investment. Hopefully, by starting a college fund early enough, you or your children will have the money necessary to further their education or to use as a tool to help them as they begin adulthood (e.g. buying a car, renting an apartment/house, etc.). Investing in a sports program may prove beneficial as your child may receive a scholarship to college because of their athleticism or become the next great athlete. Enforcing discipline early can yield better behavior and attitude later in life, especially in school and the work environments where a person's behavior and attitude can determine how far one goes in life or what one achieves. Regardless of what you do or how you parent, weighing out the possible long-term effects of your present actions should be at the forefront of your thinking, guiding your actions and parental decisions.

Using this long-term perspective helped me when it came to enrolling my son in swimming lessons. As a child, I was very fearful of the water and had serious reservations about learning how to swim. My mom decided to enroll me in swimming lessons one summer when I was about ten years old. I had such a fear of the water that I was unable to learn how to swim. Needless to say, I did not learn how to swim that summer. As I got older and began to like the water, I wished I had learned how to swim so that I could do fun things such as snorkeling, water gliding, and scuba diving. So, when it came to my son, I wanted to make sure he developed a love for the water early and learned how to swim so he could partake in water activities later in life if he chose to. I enrolled him in lessons at the age of four and now he loves the water. By thinking ahead and investing early, I saw the potential return on my investment, my son not being limited by his inability to swim.

Long term investing requires the investor to not sweat the small things in life. When you are investing for the long haul, you do not consume yourself with the daily or even weekly stock prices by constantly reading the newspaper or watching television to see how your stocks and investments are performing. Long term investors realize and understand the importance of studying the patterns and behaviors of their investments before making decisions about what to do with their investment. Long term investors make decisions not based on emotions or one really good day or bad day on the stock market. They observe trends, seek counsel by listening to financial advisors, and then make an informed decision about their investments.

In rearing children, parents cannot always allow the small things that happen to children dictate how they parent in the future. It is helpful for parents to observe trends and patterns in their children before making decisions that can have a lasting effect on them. For example, if your child gets hurt one time playing a sport, you should not immediately withdraw him or her from the team or sport. Bruises and bumps are a part of growing up. It would be irrational, in my opinion, for a parent to discontinue a sport over a small injury, especially if the child enjoys it. Now, if the child continually gets hurt, then a parent may want to consider stopping the sport. Or how about this example. Your child displays model behavior at school for three months and then has one bad day at school. It would be irrational, in my opinion, to call and set up a meeting with his or her teacher to discuss your child's behavior over one bad day at school. If the undesirable behavior continues, then it would be more rational to talk to the teacher. As parents, we must not let trivial, inconsistent behavior be the basis for the decisions we make regarding our children. Again, the idea is to observe trends, ask questions, and then make decisions based on facts rather than engage in knee jerk reactions driven by our emotions.

Lastly, long term investments require the investor to be open-minded. To be open minded, one must be willing, at the very least, to listen to new or alternative ideas, concepts, and ways of thinking. An open-minded person is not afraid to embrace change. In investing, it is easy to stick with what you already know versus taking a leap of faith and trying something new. The unknown can be risky and no one wants to take a chance on losing some or all of their money. This concept holds true in parenting as well. When viewing children as an investment, parents who are open minded embrace the changes their children go through, practice acceptance when children fall short of our expectations, and believe there are numerous ways to parent children effectively to get the greatest return on their investment. Open minded parents tend to not adhere to strict rules, regulations, and standards. They acknowledge their way of thinking is not the only way of thinking nor is it necessarily the best mode of thinking. They are open to suggestions from others and are not consumed with doing the same things that have already been done in the past.

Just as parents should be open minded, others who work with children must be flexible in their thinking. What do I mean when I say flexible in thinking? Flexible thinking is the ability to change directions, change your focus when needed in order to find new ways of solving a problem. Children will not all act or do things the same way. Children will not always behave or perform as they should. They will engage in the unexpected. They will make mistakes. Therefore, watching over your investment requires flexible thinking to manage difficult or uncertain seasons and periods of trials and tribulations. Flexible thinking allows you to weather the storms of the terrible 2s and 3s to the dreaded teenage years. Are you able or willing to flex your thinking? Getting a return on your investment depends on it.

Chapter 2: Investing in Physical Health: Nutrition and Exercise

A friend of mine was having a conversation with a six-year old boy she was babysitting at her house. The boy was a bit on the heavy side for a six-year old, but he was still full of energy and loved playing outside. It was around dinner time and my friend was in the kitchen beginning to prepare dinner for herself and the boy. She called him in from outside and asked him what he would like for dinner. The little boy, who was slightly out of breath from running, politely answered he wanted food from one of the local fast food restaurants. My friend told the boy she was going to cook something at home, not eat out. The boy was surprised and did not know what he wanted my friend to cook. Unbeknown to my friend, fast food was a way of life for this little boy. Most of this boy's nourishment came from fast food. His mother rarely prepared home cooked meals due to her work schedule and relied on fast food to quench hunger. Well, my friend did not take him to get fast food. Instead, she cooked a meal at home and the little boy reluctantly, but surprisingly, ate it all his food.

This scenario is often too common now in many family households. It seems as if every minute of our lives is scheduled with some appointment, meeting, extra-curricular activity, errand to run, or place to be. Families are on the go more than ever. As a result, fast food has become the favored alternative in some households when there is not enough time to prepare a home cooked meal. The increased indulgence of fast food along with a sedentary lifestyle and other unhealthy eating habits has led to a rise in the childhood obesity rates in America.

According to the Center for Disease Control and Prevention (CDC), childhood obesity has more than tripled since the 1970s with about 1 out of 5 school aged children between the ages of 6-19 being defined as obese. There's a difference between being overweight and being obese. Overweight is defined as having excess body weight in relation to body height. Obesity is defined as having excess body fat. Children are considered overweight when their body mass index is at or above the 85th percentile when compared to other children of the same sex and age. Children are considered obese when their body mass index is at or above the 95th percentile when compared to children of the same sex and gender. Genetics, metabolism, environmental factors, social and individual psychology, eating habits, and the level of physical activity are factors that contribute to childhood obesity.

Childhood obesity not only affects a child's physical health, but also a child's social and emotional health. Children with obesity have a greater risk of developing chronic health problems and diseases such as asthma, sleep apneas, bone and joint problems, and type 2 diabetes when compared to their normal weight peers. The probability of bullying increases in children with obesity, which can lead to emotional and mental disorders such as depression, social isolation, and lower self-esteem. In the long-term, childhood obesity can lead to obesity in adulthood, causing heart disease, type 2 diabetes, and several types of cancer.[2] There can also be academic consequences of obesity such as decreased cognitive functioning. Research has shown children with obesity have decreased attention and memory and decision-making skills along with decreased inhibition control and delayed gratification (which may be one cause of their overeating). In the classroom, these cognitive behaviors manifest themselves in decreased academic achievement.

Too Much of a Good Thing

As parents, we have the responsibility of ensuring our children take care of their physical health to have a successful future. It is our job to manage what and how much our children eat and to make sure they are getting the physical activity they need to maintain a balanced and healthy lifestyle. Establishing healthy eating habits and maintaining physical activity begin early in a child's life. One way to establish healthy eating habits is by exhibiting healthy eating habits ourselves. Often times, child's eating habits are a reflection of what and how parents eat. Most times, adults have control over their food choices. Adults can make the conscious decision to snack on fruits and vegetables or snack on potato chips and cookies. Adults can determine how much food is necessary to satisfy their hunger. One may decide to eat a whole pint of ice cream or just one scoop. And adults can control what foods to cook for meals as well as how to prepare meals in a healthier way. As an example, one may decide to cook French fries in a deep fryer using shortening or bake French fries in the oven as a healthier alterative to frying. However, children are not privy to the same decision-making choices. Often times, children are at the mercy of what adults give them. They do not always have the luxury of getting to decide what to eat, how to prepare it, or even how much to eat. Those decisions are made for them by the adults in their lives.

Protecting our greatest investment means investing in our children's physical health and well-being. Therefore, we must make conscientious decisions regarding what we feed our children and how much physical activity they receive. Although it may be more convenient to grab breakfast, lunch, or dinner from the nearest fast food restaurant or more cost efficient to buy "junk food" over fresh fruits and vegetables, it is imperative parents find a means to incorporate healthy eating habits into their and their children's daily routine. A well-balanced diet contains a healthy proportion of fruits, vegetables, protein, and grain. "Junk food" is defined as foods that are high in calories and low in nutritional value and are generally characterized as either snack foods or fast foods. Junk food leads to overeating because it has a high palatability rating, meaning it tastes good and is pleasing to the palate.

However, the flip side of junk food being palatable is it is high in sugar and fat content and low in fiber, offering no nutritional value.

One way to combat junk food is to limit access to and the need for junk food. If junk food is not in the home to consume, then children will not be able to consume it at will or have junk food as a choice for a snack. Therefore, buying healthy snacks instead of those loaded with fat and sugar is one way to limit access to junk food. Children can only consume food in the home they have access to. So, as parents, it is up to us to make better choices when it comes to the types of food that we bring into our homes (i.e. fast food, junk food, lower calorie snacks, fruits and vegetables) so that our children have better food choices. Another way to combat the need for junk food is to be more intentional about preparing home cooked meals. This may mean utilizing crock pot meals more so that you can prepare meals while you sleep or not at home or cooking larger quantities of food so that you have left overs for 2-3 days. The goal is for healthier eating to become a lifestyle, not just something you do one or two times a week. A life style change does not happen over-night, but a life style change will not happen unless you take the necessary steps to make it happen.

Thanks to legislation instituted by the Food and Drug Administration (FDA), restaurants are now required to label the caloric intake of their menu items. Therefore, consumers can see just how many calories are in their favorite combo meal, salad or entrée. And you will be surprised to see that something as seemingly as health as a salad is actually loaded with calories once you had the bacon, salad dressing, the croutons, etc. Equipped with this information, parents can make more informed choices when it comes to what they and their children eat. I am appreciative of this information and was amazed at how many calories I was consuming at my favorite restaurants for one meal. Some meals were upwards of 1000+ calories! That is more than half of the recommended calories an individual should consume in a day. Knowing the caloric intake of foods has caused me to think twice about ordering a meal that contains high amounts of calories and opting for lower calorie options instead or choosing different restaurants with lower calorie items altogether.

Healthy eating habits are not limited to home and restaurant environments. Child care facilities and schools play a role in establishing and maintaining healthy eating habits. Schools and daycares can assist in maintaining healthy eating habits by employing practices that promote healthy lifestyles. Some daycares and schools have adopted the farm to table or soil to spoon concept where they cook food grown in their own cultivated gardens. The produce grown in their garden is used to cook healthy, delicious meals and snacks. This reduces the amount of food children are exposed to with various chemicals and pesticides, making food safer and cleaner to eat and eliminates the use of additives and preservatives, which are added to foods to preserve taste and flavor. Since the farm to table concept allows children to consume fruits and vegetables that are fresh rather than canned, there is no need to consume the additives and preservatives found in canned foods. Other daycares and schools are providing organic food options to children.

Some restaurants have gotten in on the concept of clean eating and have adopted a farm to table approach, only using "clean" (without preservatives, additives, hormones, etc.) ingredients in their dishes. Some restaurant chains promote the use of meats such as chicken or beef from chickens and cows that are grass fed only. They claim to not use animals that have been injected with hormones to increase their size. I went to a restaurant one time. It was one of those places where you could see the food you were ordering as you ordered it. I had just ordered my vegetables and watched the server place two vegetables on my plate. When it came time to order my meat, I was going to order the chicken until I saw how big the legs and wings were. The chicken pieces were extremely large and I was afraid to eat any of it. I walked by the chicken and ordered the tilapia instead. By the size of the chicken, I knew it had been injected with something to increase its size. Whatever it was, I did not want it inside of me! After that experience, I have never eaten at that restaurant again.

Why are additives and preservatives bad to consume? Through research, additives and preservatives have been shown to cause heart damage, behavioral and mood changes, breathing difficulties, and cancer. Additives and preservatives are also found in sodas, salad dressing, snack food, and processed meats. Common additives and preservatives are BHT/BHA, sulfites, sodium benzoate, and nitrite. Look for these names when you read the ingredient labels on the foods you eat.

Let's not forget the beverages children drink. What children drink is as equally important as what they eat. Sodas, energy drinks, frappuccino and lattes, and some juices contain high amounts of calories, sugar, and preservatives. Fruit juice can be deceptive in its overall health benefits. Although research shows drinking fruit juice is still healthier than drinking soda, fruit juice is not without its limitations. One problem with most fruit juices is that they lose their nutritional value the longer they sit on a shelf without being consumed. Companies use various methods of storage that can allow them to store juice for up to a year. One such method removes oxygen from the liquid. Once the oxygen is removed from the liquid, it is then stored in tanks until it is packaged in cartons, placed on a delivery truck, stocked on a grocery store shelf, and stored in our refrigerators. Secondly, the additives and preservatives companies place in juice to extend their shelf life or to add flavor reduces the nutritional value of the juice. Therefore, the nutritional information reported on the juice (which is labeled according to the nutritional value at the time of processing the juice) is different from the actual nutritional value at the time the consumer buys the product.

In addition, the amount of sugar found in foods and beverages is another contributing factor to the rise in childhood obesity. The most common forms of sugar are sucrose (regular table sugar) and high fructose corn syrup (HFCS). High fructose corn syrup is a sweetener made from corn starch that is chemically similar to regular sugar (sucrose), which is made from sugar cane or sugar beet. Table sugar is comprised of 50% glucose and 50% fructose. HFCS is comprised of approximately 45% glucose and 55% fructose. HFCS is added to a variety of food and drinks such as soda, ice cream/yogurt, fruit juices, salad dressings, energy drinks, candy, boxed dinners, processed foods, bread, breakfast cereal, store-bought baked goods, jams/jellies, junk food, and sauces and condiments such as ketchup and mustard. HFCS is widely used because it is cheaper and is perceived as sweeter than regular cane or beet sugar. When fructose is consumed, the body metabolizes it in the liver and the liver generally converts the fructose to glycogen (stored fat). When glucose is consumed, it is metabolized in the cells of the body to provide energy for organs and muscles. Small amounts of fructose found in fruits and vegetables are converted to glucose; however, large amounts of fructose found in soft drinks and candy bars are converted to fat. Excess fat in the body leads to weight gain and associated health problems. As a result, too much of either one (sucrose or HFCS) is not good for the body.

Since HFCS has gotten a reputation for contributing to increased health problems such as type 2 diabetes, obesity and heart disease, many food companies have removed this ingredient from their products. Now, the words "no high fructose corn syrup" are clearly labeled on food items to let the consumer know. When it comes to investing in our children's physical health, following the guidelines set forth by the American Heart Association (AHA) can assist parents in monitoring their children's sugar intake. According to the AHA, preschool children should not consume more than 170 calories or 4 teaspoons of sugar per day. The intake goes up to 6 teaspoons a day for older children. The AHA recommends children under the age of two not consume any foods or drinks with added sugar.[3] One teaspoon of sugar is equal to four grams of sugar. So, children should not consume more than 16-24 grams of sugar (sucrose or HFCS) per day. The average 20-ounce soda bottle has approximately 70 grams of sugar and an average 8- ounce bottle of apple or orange juice has approximately 25 grams of sugar.[4] The bottom line is we as parents must be vigilant about the food and beverages our children consume by reading the nutritional labels on foods and drinks and opting for healthier choices such as eating more fruits and vegetables, drinking more water, eating less fast food, and consuming lower calorie food and beverage.

In addition to the sugar found in food, we must be conscious of the fat found in foods. Not all fat found in food is bad for us. Good fats such as monounsaturated and polyunsaturated fats are a source of energy for the body and aid the body in absorbing vitamins and minerals. They are needed for muscle movement and blood clotting and are found in vegetables, nuts, fish, cooking oils (canola, peanut, olive) and seeds. They remain in liquid form at room temperature. Trans-unsaturated fatty acids (aka trans fat or trans fatty acids), a man-made fat, is considered bad fat. Saturated fat falls somewhere between the good fats (monounsaturated and polyunsaturated fats) and the bad fat (trans fat). Saturated fat is found in food such as red meat, whole milk, cheese, and commercially prepared foods. Saturated fat becomes solid at room temperature (e.g. bacon grease) and can lead to blockage in the arteries of the heart and other organs. Therefore, it is recommended we limit our daily consumption of saturated fat to less than 10% of our daily caloric intake.[5]

    Trans fat are a byproduct of a process called hydrogenation, which uses hydrogen to turn healthy oils into solids, keeping the oil from spoiling. This process turns the healthy vegetable oil into unhealthy oil. When consumed in the body, trans fat increases the level of bad cholesterol in the body and decreases the level of good cholesterol in the body. As a result, trans fat increases the risk of health conditions such as stroke, diabetes, heart disease and other chronic conditions. On nutritional labels, you might see "partially hydrogenated oil" listed as an ingredient. If you do see these words, then it is trans fat and a food to avoid or limit consumption.

Similar to HFCS, trans fat is used commonly in processed foods and restaurants because of its affordability, how long it can last, and the desired taste and texture it adds to foods. Trans fat can be found in foods such as frozen pizza, fried foods, and baked goods (cakes, cookies). Due to the increased risk of health conditions associated with consuming trans fat, the AHA recommends eliminating, or at least reducing, the amount of trans fat in our diets. By eating more fruits and vegetables, cooking food in healthy oils, decreasing daily consumption of red meat, food and drinks high in sugar, consuming foods prepared without "partially hydrogenated oils" or "hydrogenated oils," and reading the nutritional labels on food items, we as parents can take an active role in what we offer our children for meals and snacks. The next time you are grocery shopping or deciding what items to eat from a menu, take a moment and read the label. You will be amazed at the amount of fat that is lurking in the foods you eat.

The Power of Movement

So far, the conversation has been about establishing and maintaining healthy eating habits. Yet, eating healthy is not enough to maintain a healthy lifestyle. Investing in our children's physical health also requires ensuring they receive adequate physical activity. The CDC recommends children receive at least 60 minutes of physical activity a day. Children do not need continuous 60 minutes of physical activity. 60 minutes can be accomplished throughout the day in smaller increments that add up to 60 minutes. The goal is to participate in at least 60 minutes of physical activity per day. Physical activity comes in many shapes and form. Physical activity includes activities such as biking, walking, running, swimming, jogging, dancing, yoga, and playing sports.

A friend and I were talking one day about how much children of today differ from children of our generation. We could remember going outside to play games with our friends. Staying outside until the street lights came on. Riding bikes throughout the neighborhood. And walking from house to house to play with the neighborhood kids. Then, she told me about an encounter she had with a young teacher who was in her early twenties. The young teacher entered my friend's classroom and noticed an interesting image drawn on her floor. The image was a configuration of squares with numbers in them. Some of the squares were horizonal while others were vertical. "What is that?" the young teacher asked. Can you guess what the young teacher saw? If you guessed hop scotch, you guessed correctly. The young teacher was looking at a hop scotch diagram on the floor. She had no idea what it was and to my friend's amazement, she responded "Hopscotch."

My friend was baffled at the fact the young teacher did not know what a hopscotch game was. The young teacher began asking questions about how the game is played. My friend explained the rules of the game to the naïve teacher. The next day, the young teacher drew a similar hopscotch game on her classroom floor and incorporated the game into her lesson with her students. The class had fun learning and playing hopscotch. The young teacher was grateful to my friend for sharing with her the game of hopscotch. The point of this story is to shed light on how far society has come from young children playing outdoors with friends to preferring the lights and sounds of social media, smartphones, videogames, and computers. These gadgets have taken the place of good old-fashioned outdoor fun.

The "Let's Move" campaign initiated by former first lady of the United States, Michelle Obama, was a collaborative effort by families, schools, and communities to reduce childhood obesity. The campaign aimed to combat childhood obesity by encouraging healthy eating habits and physical activity in the home, school, and community environments. The appeal of "Let's Move" prompted the US Tennis Association to build or repair over 6200 kid-sized tennis courts throughout the country and the Blue Cross Blue Shield Association to fund the initiation of 40 "play street" (streets without traffic) across the United States where children and families could enjoy outdoor activities such as walking, biking, or running.

The benefits of physical activity are numerous. Physical activity reduces the amount of fat in the body, builds muscle, relieves stress, promotes bone and joint development, and decreases the risk of developing health conditions such as diabetes, heart disease, and high blood pressure. In addition, it aids in brain health development and functioning, helping children perform better in school.

Physical Activity and Academic Performance

There is a growing body of research suggesting physical activity improves academic performance in schools by increasing cognitive functions such as attention and memory skills. Good attention and memory skills are essential for learning. When children are focused on the topic at hand, they are able to better retain the information. Reading and math are the subjects that benefit the most from increased physical activity. However, the type of physical activity is important. Research suggests the more vigorous the physical activity (e.g. running, jumping) is, the better the effects on attention and memory skills. Less vigorous physical activities such as walking or doing push-ups still produces increases in attention and memory; however, the increase is not as significant as it is with more vigorous forms of activity.

However, in today's technologically advanced society, children are exposed to iPads, smart phones, and other electronic gadgets early in life with limited exposure to outdoor play and activities. There was a time, at least when I was growing up, when children looked forward to going outside to play games such as "Red light. Green light. Stop," "Mother, "May I...," "Duck Duck Goose," dodge ball, and a host of other outdoor games. Nowadays, children do not know what to do when they have to go outside. Going outside is more of a chore than an activity they look forward to doing. Children are accustomed to being inside watching television and/or playing video games. We, as a society (or as parents), must get back to the time when our lives were not consumed with social media and electronic gadgets and foster outdoor activities. Our sedentary lifestyles are slowly debilitating us.

With today's busy schedules, it can feel almost impossible to engage in 60 minutes of rigorous physical activity each day. Making time for physical activity requires parents to adopt the long-term perspective of investing. As parents, we must realize the benefits of physical activity and its impact on not only our children's bodies, but also their minds. We must examine the long-term effects of developing habits of physical activity in children. Here are a few suggestions of how to incorporate more physical activity in not only our children's lives, but also our own lives. We, as parents, must lead by example. When our children see us engaged in physical activity, they are more likely to engage in physical activity as well. We cannot adopt the mantra "Do as I say, not as I do" and expect to be effective in our efforts to increase physical activity in our children. Nor can we as parents be slack in our efforts to get more physical activity. Again, we model for our children what we value by the actions, or lack of, we take. Remember, it is not how vigorous the activity is. It is the amount of time spent doing the activity and how consistent you are in completing the activity.

Incorporating Physical Activity
1. Go for family walks after meals.
2. Park farther away from store entrances so that you have to walk more.
3. Use the stairs instead of the elevator.
4. Engage in household chores (e.g. vacuuming, washing dishing, folding clothes, etc.) and/or yard work (e.g. raking leaves, planting flowers, etc.).
5. Dance to your favorite songs.
6. Wash a car by hand.
7. Actively play with pets or take them for walks.
8. Go to the park and play more (throw a frisbee or ball, play tag, fly a kite, etc.)
9. Ride bikes.
10. Go bowling or skating.
11. Walk around while talking on the phone.
12. Practice shooting, passing, and dribbling a basketball.
13. Practice kicking a soccer ball.
14. Do jumping jacks or other exercises.
15. Walk around the neighborhood.

Physical Activity and Emotional Health

Physical activity is not just associated with increased cognitive abilities, but also with improved emotional health. When we possess good emotional health, we are in control of what we think, what we do, and what we say. Emotional health is essential for proper functioning in life. Being able to cope with the stresses and problems of life as well as possessing the resilience needed to bounce back from life's problems are necessary components for successful living. Good emotional health promotes these abilities. Research shows physical activity such as yoga, exercise, sports, etc. has been shown to reduce stress, anxiety, and mental fatigue, increase energy levels, promote better sleep, and encourage a positive self-image. In other words, physical activity improves not only physical health, but emotional health too!

When the body perceives a stressful event such as when you hear a sudden loud noise, or when a large dog is chasing you, or when you are taking a test, it produces two hormones; adrenaline and cortisol. Adrenaline increases your heart rate, blood pressure, and energy supply. Cortisol, which is the primary stress hormone, increases glucose levels in the blood and temporarily suspends the functions of the immune system, digestive system, reproductive system, and growth process. Cortisol also communicates with the brain to help regulate our moods, motivation, and fear. A stressful event can be any physical, emotional, or mental situation the body perceives as a threat to the body's equilibrium. When the perceived stressful event is gone or eliminated, the adrenaline and cortisol levels of the body return back to their normal levels and bodily systems return back to their normal functioning.

However, when the body is placed under stress for extended periods of time, it overproduces the hormones cortisol and adrenaline. The excess production of cortisol and adrenaline can lead to anxiety, depression, digestive problems, headaches, weight gain, sleep problems, heart disease, and decreased cognitive functioning. Regular physical activity helps to regulate the release of cortisol in the body to decrease the chance of weight gain, mood swings, and to increase motivational levels. Therefore, when we invest in our children's physical health, we are investing in maintaining their emotional health.

Physical activity also increases the production of endorphin in the body. Endorphins are neurotransmitters in the body that transmit electrical signals within the nervous system. Endorphins elicit the feelings of euphoria or happiness in the body and are released in the body as a response to pain to function as the body's natural painkiller. The release of endorphins is associated with changes in one's mood and lowers the occurrence of depression. Rigorous physical activity is just one way to release endorphins in the body. With children as our greatest investment, we must make the time to encourage more physical activity.

Chapter 3: Investing in Emotional Health: Part 1
How do you parent?

When my son was born, my husband and I had the privilege to attend parenting classes offered at our church. The classes were designed for new parents, parents with children, and parents who just needed help with their children. There were several parents in our class. Some were new parents like us. Others had multiple children of various ages, ranging from newborn to teenagers. During one of the classes, we had a discussion describing the type of household we grew up in, whether it was a loving, caring household, or a household without boundaries, or a strict household, or a household with a substance abuser, etc. In comparing my experience to others, it was interesting to hear how diverse some people were raised. Some parents in the class were raised with very strict rules while other had no rules at all. Some parents were raised in loving, affectionate households while others were reared in household where love and affection were not shown.

    I think, at times, we tend to assume most people were brought up in a household similar to our own. Anything contrary to that seems unfathomable, strange, or different. This is a revelation I gained during the first year of my undergraduate experience. Some people were brought up in very lenient households where they were able to do pretty much what they wanted (within reason). Some were brought up in very strict homes where they were not allowed to participate in many outside activities or activities that resembled fun. Some were disciplined while others lack rules and consequences for behavior. Some grew up in households with little to no affection shown. No hugs or kisses good night and there was definitely no verbal expression of "I love you." Yet other households were openly affectionate.

The reason I am sharing this with you is that most, if not all of those in attendance, were there because we wanted to parent our children differently from the way we were parented or wanted new ideas on how to parent our children in order to cultivate the best in our children. The fact is children are not born with a manual full of dos and don'ts to raise successful children. Most of us parent the way we were parented because that is all we know to do. We follow the examples of our mothers and fathers and make changes as we see fit for our own children. If you were spanked, then you may be more prone to spank your children or the opposite may be true. Because you were spanked, you may decide not to spank your children. If your mom or dad was not affectionate with you, you may not be apt to show affection to your children or being in a less affectionate household may prompt you slather your children with hugs and kisses. If you were encouraged and told you could do whatever you wanted, then you are more than likely going to instill those same beliefs and values in your children. There are no right or wrong ways to parent, but there are better ways to parent. I am not saying we cannot learn how to parent based on the way we were parented. We can certainly learn from our parents' or others' successes and failures. I am simply suggesting, as the famed poet Maya Angelou stated, "Do the best you can until you know better. Then when you know better, do better."

Investing in our children also means ensuring their emotional health and well-being as well as their educational success is intact. How we parent children is critical in determining the kind of return we want on our investment, our children. Research has shown parenting styles, parental practices, and parental involvement are key factors that have influential impact on a child's educational and emotional success.[6,7] One researcher defined parenting styles as "the emotional climate in which parents raise their children" and is associated with the demandingness and the responsiveness of parents. [6] Let's further talk about demandingness and responsiveness.

Demandingness refers to the expectations and demands parents place on their children to help integrate them into the family and society and are related to educational achievement, performance, and behavior. Demandingness can be thought of as the requirements parents have of their children. As a parent, do you require obedience? Respect? Kindness? Honesty? Doing chores? Getting good grades? Manners? These demands and expectations, or lack thereof, help children successfully or unsuccessfully function within their environment (e.g. school, home, church, social, community, etc.).

Responsiveness refers to how well parents intentionally promote autonomy and independence, emotional/psychological well-being, and self-regulation of emotions and behaviors in their children.[6] Responsiveness can be thought of in terms of a parent's response to his/her child's thoughts, words, actions, and behaviors. As a parent, do you comfort your child via hugs, kisses, and kind words? Or do you curse at them, call them harsh names such as "stupid" and "lazy" and respond with physical actions? Do you allow your children to make their own choices? Or do you tell them what to do, when to do it, where to do it, who to do it with, and how to do it? Do you encourage or berate your child when he/she does something wrong? We will discuss the impact of demandingness and responsiveness and how they relate to the educational and emotional development in children later in this chapter. But first, let's take a look at the different parenting styles.

Parenting Styles

Based on research conducted by developmental psychologist, Diana Baumrind, parenting styles can be categorized into four categories: authoritative, authoritarian, permissive, and neglectful.

These parenting classifications have been around since the 1960s and are still widely used today by psychologist to describe parental interactions with their children.[8] The first parenting style I will discuss is the authoritative parenting style.

Authoritative parenting is characterized by warmth, low parental/psychological control, high parental care, and democracy. Authoritative parents place high maturity expectations on their children, are responsive to their needs, and exercise control over their behavior. They provide the emotional support and autonomy needed to make choices related to their children's interests. Two-way communication exists between the parent and child regarding expectations and the rationale for expectations.[6,9] Children, whose parents practice an authoritative parenting style, tend to possess a happy disposition, are confident about their abilities, are able to effectively manage their emotions during emotional experiences for socially acceptable responses, and have good social skills.

Authoritative parents also ensure their children's day has structure such as designated bed and/or meal times. They set reasonable expectations for their children and share them with their children so their children know what is expected of them. They also employ consequences for inappropriate behavior with explanations of why the behavior is inappropriate. In addition, authoritative parents maintain open communication with their children. They provide an atmosphere where the child feels comfortable enough to discuss difficult or important issues without the fear of shame or disapproval from their parents. This is probably the most important trait for authoritative parents to demonstrate. Let's see why that is.

As children progress into middle and high school ages, they begin to face more and more peer pressure from friends and other students to engage in activities such as alcohol, drugs, sex. During the middle school years, children begin to make social comparisons within their peer groups and the need for peer acceptance becomes more crucial in their socio-emotional development and can affect their future academic success. As a result, children may engage in behaviors contradictory to their upbringing as a way to fit in within their peer group.

According to developmental psychologist Erik Erickson's, stages of psychosocial behavior, as children get older, they become less dependent on guidance from their parents in determining who they are and seek validation and an understanding of themselves through their peers. In other words, instead of identifying with their parent's beliefs, children typically start to gravitate towards the behaviors, attitudes, and values of their friends and fellow students. So, it is crucial parents are aware of whom their children are hanging around and who their friends are. Therefore, it is important for children to feel safe when talking with their parents, especially as they progress into middle and high school. Our children need to feel as if they can share their thoughts, feelings, and experiences with us. For this reason, two-way communication provides an avenue for children to speak openly with their parents and allows parents the ability to maintain some impact on the decisions their children make. An authoritative parenting style allows for the important two-way communication needed between parent and child.

The second type of parenting style is the authoritarian. Authoritarian parenting is characterized by high demands and expectations of children, but with little warmth (emotional support) or responsiveness to their children's needs. Authoritarian parents expect strict obedience of rules, without providing rationales, and exert parental/psychological control over their children's actions and behaviors. Authoritarian parents are known as "strict" parents. Little or no two-way communication between the parent and child exists.[6] When questioned by their children, often times, the authoritarian parent's response is "because I said so." No rationale for a response is given for following rules. Punishment is the primary means authoritarian parents use to get their children to follow the rules. They have a do this or else attitude. Authoritarian parents offer little or no opportunities for their children to make their own decisions. These are the parents that say "my son is going to play football/basketball." Or "my child is going to a four- year institution." Or "my daughter is not participating in beauty pageants." Their children have little or no voice in making decisions about their own lives.

In addition to the strict rules and intrusive decision making, authoritarian parents provide little to no emotional support to their children. They do not demonstrate affection via hugs, kisses, a pat on the back or through kind words. As a result, children of authoritarian parents may appear anxious, withdrawn, and unhappy, become hostile or quickly give up when frustrated. On the other hand, these children are less likely to engage in activities such as drug or alcohol abuse and gangs and tend to perform well in school. They are able to avoid the pitfalls of gangs, premarital sex, and truancy and maintain good grades out of fear of their parents and the punishment associated with not following the rules or meeting expectations.

For these reasons, an authoritarian parenting style may not seem that bad. However, research on the long-term effects of authoritarian parenting yielded adults who were less socially competent than their peers. Children who come from homes with high parental control also tend to exhibit greater emotional suppression in adolescence and decreased emotional regulation in early adulthood. In other words, these children, when they become adults, are less likely to express their emotions and are more likely to have difficulty with managing their emotions appropriately in response to emotional experiences. Emotions affect our cognitive and mental state, thus affecting our decision-making abilities. Having emotional wellbeing, responding appropriately to life events, is pertinent to effective decision making in adolescence and adulthood and begins in childhood.

Permissive parenting is characterized by low or no maturity demands and expectations placed on children and more tolerance of misbehavior. Although permissive parents display warmth and emotional support for their children, they exert little or no parental/psychological control over their child's behavior.[8] Permissive parents provide few, if any, consequences for their children's misbehavior. Children of permissive parents lack structure in their daily routines, rules to govern their behavior, and boundaries. The lack of structure, rules, and boundaries can lead to children who are less self-disciplined and self-controlled. These children are sometimes seen as "brats" or "spoiled" because they feel their environment and those in it (e.g. parents, teachers, siblings, friends, other family members) revolve around their wants and needs. Children of permissive parenting can become defiant and rebellious when their desires are challenged by someone in a position of authority. Additionally, children from permissive households do not persist in the face of difficult challenges. They are easy to give up when things become challenging.

When permissive parents do impose rules, boundaries, and structure, they are generally temporary and/or inconsistently applied. A new rule or structure may last for a week and then it is back to the usual routine. As a result, permissive parents are often viewed as lenient, a "push over," or wanting to be their child's friend. Permissive parents also parent according to their child's mood and use bribery as a means of managing behavior. They avoid confronting their children's misbehavior in an effort not to upset their children.

In an attempt to evade the harsh authoritarian parenting style imposed upon them as children, parents from authoritarian upbringing will sometimes adopt a permissive parenting style in response to their authoritarian upbringing. Permissive parenting may appear to be the choice of children because of the lack of rules and boundaries used, but it has damaging long-term effects on children as they become adults. Studies concerning adolescents and teens suggest some of the long-term effects include more indulgence in underage drinking, self-centeredness, poor academic success caused by a lack of motivation to achieve, poor social skills (e.g. sharing, taking turns) due to a lack of discipline, and conflicts with authority. These behaviors have root in the lack of rules and the lack of consequences for not following the rules associated with a permissive household. Contrary to what some parents may believe or think, young children desire structure and boundaries in their environment. Structure and boundaries make children feel safe because they are aware of the limitations of their behavior and the child and parental roles are clearly defined. Going outside of their boundaries or imposed structure represents a sense of danger or unsafety while remaining inside the constraints of boundaries and rules represent a sense of safety.

The last and most damaging parenting style is neglectful or involved parenting. As the name suggests, neglectful parenting is characterized by willingly or unwillingly neglecting the physical, emotional/mental, and/or educational needs of the child. They are viewed as unresponsive and emotionally "cold." Neglectful parents may not take their children to the doctor for regular checkups, follow-up with homework or school assignments, provide a safe, clean, healthy home environment for children to thrive, or show no emotional support for their children. Neglectful parents are unaware of what is going on in their children's lives. They do not know who their children associate with or their activities in and outside of school. They do not know who their teachers are at school or what grades they are receiving in school. Often times, children of neglectful parents are left alone to take care of themselves or their siblings. Neglectful parents tend to make excuses for why they do not spend more time with their children at home. Children of neglectful parenting have difficulty developing trust and forming relationships with their parents or other people, display impulsive behaviors, are delinquent at school, and have a higher chance of engaging in high risk behaviors such as alcohol and drugs. Sometimes, neglectful parents may have drug or alcohol problems themselves, leaving their children to take care of them.

To assist you in identifying your parenting style, I have included a diagram on the next page to help you identify the differences among the four parenting styles along with general characteristic of each one. Knowing what parenting style you adopt is crucial in maximizing the return on your investment, your children. The expectations and demands you place on children along with the amount of emotional support you provide are critical elements in the development of children into adults. Your parenting style affects the future choices and decisions your child makes and influences the kind of adult your child will become. As parents, it is important to remember we are not simply rearing children. We are rearing children so that they are able to function appropriately in their environment and in society as adults.

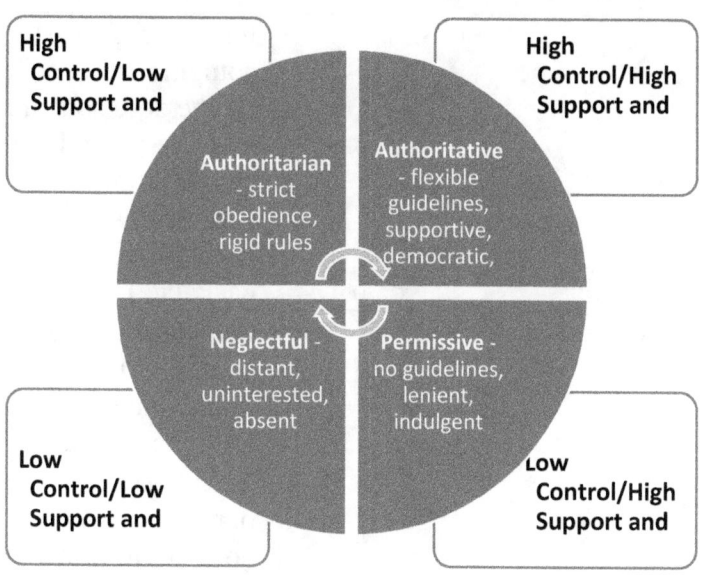

General Parenting Style Characteristics

Parenting Style	Parental Characteristics
Authoritative	<ul><li>Parent listens attentively to child</li><li>Parent reasons with child in stead of being demamding or forceful</li><li>Parent gives child the freedom to make his/her own choices in life</li><li>Parent consitently sets and enforces well-defined boundaries, limits, and expectations</li><li>Parent uses positive disciplinary techniques rather than degrading or embarrassing ones</li><li>Parent encourages independence</li><li>Parent nutures child through warm, comforting</li></ul>

	interactions such as complimenting child when he/she does something well, using respectful tone in conversation, and expressions of love (i.e. hugs, kisses, pats on the back, etc.)
Authoritarian	• Parent sets and expects child to follow a strict set of rules, some which maybe unspoken or unexplained • Parent uses harsh punishments when child does not follow rules • Parent engages in cold, unloving interactions with child (i.e. no show of love via hugs, kisses, etc.) • Parent provides feedback to child often times in the form of yelling or nagging the child with little or no encouraging and/or comforting words • Parent is intolerant of child's undesired behaviors • Parent does not give child the freedom of choice when it comes to managing his/her life; little to no negotiating with child • Parent uses shame and embarrassment to control child's behavior
Permissive	• Parent sets very few rules, limits, boundaries, and expectations of child. • Parent engages in warm,

	• loving interactions with child such as expressions of love and compliments.
• Parent is inconsistent with enforcing rules when child does not follow them or consequences when child behaves inappropriately
• Parent considers child's opinion and feelings when making decisions regarding child.
• Parent uses bribery (i.e. promise of gifts, toys, money, etc.) to mangage child's behavior.
• Parent does not hold child accountable for inappropriate behavior.
• Parent provides child with little or no structure or schedule at home.
Neglectful	• Parent displays no affection, love or warmth towards child.
• Parent is more concerned about his/her own welfare (i.e life circumstances) and does not consider the welfare of the child.
• Parent offers little or no supervison of child's behavior or actions; therefore, there are no consequences for inappropriate behavior.
• Parent has little or no expectation regarding child's behavior or actions.

	• Parent in uninvolved in child's educational needs.

Often times, our parenting style seeps over into other ways we interact and engage with children such as the way we teach students in our classroom, the way we counsel children, or the way we coach players on our team. Our approach to handling children and youth behavior and performance has roots in one of the four parenting styles. We can be a very strict disciplinarian in the classroom or in the locker room. Or we can be too lax with rules and expectations. Hopefully, we fall somewhere in the middle, the authoritative parenting style. It's not just parents who have an impact on children's lives, but also the other adults in their lives as well. We ALL play a part in nurturing and developing children. We ALL are making an investment in our youth.

Emotional Knowledge

Before we discuss emotional knowledge and intelligence, let's talk about what emotions are. Have you ever thought to ask yourself what are emotions? Emotions cannot be condensed down to one idea, concept, or definition. There are many facets to emotions. First of all, emotions are **subjective**. They "lead to feeing a certain way."[9] At times, our emotions are very describable and palatable, as if we can touch them. At other times, words cannot accurately express how we feel or convey our mood. Secondly, emotions are **biological.** They are "energy mobilizing response systems that prepare the body for adapting to whatever situation one faces."[9] There is a biological component to emotions. Emotions can cause bodily reactions such as increased heart rate, increased blood pressure, and an increase in body temperature in people. These biological reactions are in response to how something or someone made us feel.

Emotions are also **purposive**. They "generate urges and impulses to action."[9] Our emotions propel us to act according to how we feel, whether positive or negative. The way we respond or react to someone or something is generally related to the emotion we are feeling at the time of the event or situation. And how strongly we respond or react is directly related to how strong are emotions are at the time of the event. For example, the compassion we feel towards starving children may cause us to contribute money or food items to a local food bank or even volunteer at one. On the other hand, the feeling of betrayal you may experience after someone close to you has done something hurtful to you may cause you to want to cause harm to them in return. Lastly, emotions are **expressive**. Emotions are expressed through facial expressions, body language, posture, and vocal signals that "communicate the quality and intensity of our emotionality to others."[9] You can see when someone is happy by the smile on his or her face. You can see the look of disgust on a person's face by the snarling of his or her nose. These and other expressions relay how we are feeling without necessarily having to tell others how we are feeling.

How we parent contributes to the overall emotional well-being of our children. Protecting your greatest investment means making sure you have invested in your child's emotional health as well. Children who have emotional knowledge and intelligence tend to grow up to be well-adjusted adults. Emotional knowledge and intelligence allow children to be better equipped to cope with the stresses of life and bounce back from adversity. Having emotional knowledge and intelligence simply means children are aware of their emotions and the emotions of others. Children who possess emotional intelligence and knowledge have words to express how they feel and how someone or an event or action make them feel. They know when they have hurt someone or when someone has hurt them.

As an example, children know when mommy or daddy is pleased with their grades from school. They know when mommy or daddy is upset or disappointed about their grades from school. When children have difficulty speaking their emotions or when their emotional needs are not being met, they sometimes act out, misbehave, or display inappropriate behavior to fill an emotional void or to get an emotional need met. These are maladaptive behaviors, inappropriate ways of handling emotions, children use when they lack emotional knowledge, intelligence, and support.

Did you know children are born with the ability to show emotions from birth? Think back to when your child was first born. Think back to how your child expressed joy through laughter and smiling as you talked to him. Think back to how your child expressed disgust at a particular food you tried to feed him or her for the first time and they did not like it. Or think back to when your child's eyes widened when something scary was present or they heard a loud, unexpected noise. Even at a young age, your child was expressing emotions although they may not have had the words to label them.

Babies are born with the ability to display at least six basic emotions: sadness, joy, disgust, anger, surprise, and fear. These emotions are usually visible by watching babies' facial expressions and body language and listening to the tone of their voice. Just as mothers and fathers can distinguish between a hungry cry or a dirty diaper cry, parents can distinguish when their baby is happy, sad, scared, or disgusted by the tone of their voice or cry or their facial expressions. However, other emotions and emotional states, such as nervousness, embarrassment, anger, anxiety, calm, etc. and how to respond to them appropriately need to be taught to children. Children are not born with an innate sense of these emotions. Children develop an understanding of the less obvious emotions and emotional states by watching other people: parents, family members, siblings, friends, teachers, other children. They observe how people, especially their parental figures, respond and react to situations. By watching and being able to read others' facial expressions, body language and gestures, and vocal tone, children learn what hurt is, what embarrassment is, what jealousy is, or what being sorry is. When the adults in children's lives place labels on these emotions and behaviors, children gain more insight into social cognitive knowledge, which is understanding the connection between emotions and feelings and different situations and events.

    One example stands out in my mind that illustrates how children feel different emotions but do not possess the verbal skills to express what they are feeling. My son loves to be the center of attention no matter where we are. He is the only grandchild on my side of the family and my mother and step-father spoil him with gifts and attention. One day, when my son was about five years old, we invited several family members over to our house for a father's day meal. By chance, another little boy about my son's age was there. He and my son laughed and played right up until it was time to go. Just before the little boy was getting ready to go, he started reciting all the books of the bible. Everyone was impressed by this little boy's ability to recall all 66 books of the bible. He was showered with praise, high fives, and "good jobs" by everyone. Even I praised the little boy for how well he did.

    Off to the side, I noticed my son with his head down walking quietly upstairs by himself. I immediately knew what was wrong with him. I followed him up the stairs and asked him what was wrong. He stated no one was clapping for him and that I should only clap when he does good things because he was my son and not the other little boy. I knew he was jealous of all the attention the other little boy was receiving, yet he was unable to verbalize that emotion. I talked to him about how praising one child does not diminish our love for him and that we cannot always be the center of attention. I am not sure if he totally understood what I was saying, but I know he was processing that emotional event, the way it made him feel and his response. To this day, he remembers that event and how it made him feel. He talks about it until this day.

I am glad that my son chose not to act out in response to the little boy's attention and how the situation made him feel. He could have channeled those emotions into something negative like throwing things, saying something mean, or hitting something or someone. He chose to deal with the emotion quietly and by himself. Yet, I was there to assist him in identifying what he was feeling (jealousy) so that he would later have a name to express that emotion and an understanding of what jealousy feels like and what causes jealous emotions. I discussed the emotion and what caused the emotion with him. In that moment, I was increasing my son's emotional knowledge and intelligence.

Besides the six basic emotions children possess at birth, children learn other emotional states through their social interaction with their environment (people, and objects). An emotional event consists of an antecedent, behavioral changes, a cognitive appraisal, and a reaction or response (the emotion). Let me further explain these terms to help you better grasp the concept behind emotions. To understand emotions and mental states, one must consider the antecedent (life event) that elicited the emotion. For children, these life events could be a child taking a toy out of their hand, a parent giving a treat for doing well, falling on the floor in front friends, or a host of events that take place during the course of childhood. Emotions help us adapt to the opportunities and challenges we face during important life events.

How children appraise or assign meaning to these life events shapes how children internalize and express the emotions associated with the life event. By appraise, I am referring to how children perceive a life event or what opinion their minds form about an event. Was it a good or bad situation? Did it cause me harm? What was the benefit of this event, if any? Was there any threat in the situation? If so, what was it? These are the questions children are consciously or subconsciously asking themselves when a life event happens. The answers to these questions determine the emotional output. For example, a child falls down in front of his friends. His friends start to laugh at him. The child's body starts to react with an increased heart rate, flushed face, and increase in body temperature. He is appraising the fall in front of his friends as a bad situation, so he gets up and runs away crying. He has just experienced embarrassment. Now, the child may not know that he is embarrassed; therefore, as adults we must assign the word embarrassed to that feeling so the child is able to associate that feeling with the word embarrass. Therefore, he has the emotional knowledge to label what he has experienced and relate to the feeling of embarrassment if he reads about it in a book or hears the word in a story.

It is very simple formula. There is something that happens in our life (antecedent), next our mind forms an opinion about the event (cognitive appraisal) and our body produces a biological reaction to the event, and then we experience the associated emotion. You can explain emotions to your child, right?

Children do not innately know how to process their or other people's feelings and emotions. They require guidance (i.e. knowledge and instruction) to help them interpret what they are feeling and the emotions they are experiencing. They also need guidance in how to interact appropriately regarding others' feelings and emotions. When we teach children how to effectively express their feelings and how to appropriately respond rather than react to the emotions of others (e.g. friends, siblings, classmates, family members, etc.), we help them to better recognize and process their own feelings and emotions, as well as those of others. This ability to recognize and accurately interpret one's emotion and the emotions of others is necessary in effectively interacting with others socially and de-escalating difficult or stressful situations they encounter.

I have listed below some steps to take to help increase children's emotional knowledge and understanding. It is crucial as parents we provide children with the knowledge needed to express themselves so that children can adequately respond to situations in life. Going back to the example with my son, had I not explained to my son what he was feeling, he would not have a name to equate with the emotional experience. By doing so, I increased his emotional knowledge and provided a positive outlet for him to express his emotion.

Protecting our children means ensuring they mature into well-adjusted adults. Try these steps at home, at school, church, or wherever you interact with children and youth to help with increasing your children's emotional knowledge. I will refer to my son's example as a way for you to see the steps in action.

Step 1

Provide children with the words that represent their feelings and emotions. Begin with emotions that are easily recognizable according to facial expressions, body language, and vocal tone such as angry, sad, happy or scared. Then, move to less visibly recognizable emotions such as lonely, embarrassment, nervousness, or frustration. Teach your children about how the latter emotions make you feel inside and outside and what circumstances may cause them to feel these emotions.

When my son retreated upstairs, I started talking to him about feelings of jealousy because that was the emotion he was feeling at the time. I supplied him with the word jealous to represent what he was feeling. Even though he may not have understood what jealous meant, he knew how it felt.

Step 2

Introduce emotional concepts during story time, structured activity time (e.g. coloring, painting, making crafts, baking cookies or brownies, etc.), or play time by using pictures and facial expressions to help children better understand the connection between feelings and self-expression. Use this structured time to educate your child on emotions the characters are feeling in a story or how the characters in their favorite cartoon, movie, or television show are feeling during a coloring activity.

Even older children need help in processing their emotions, especially as they enter puberty and their hormones are constantly changing. It may not be prudent to use coloring pages, playtime, or their favorite cartoon character to discuss a teenager's feelings and emotions. They may not take you seriously. But providing a safe environment, one free of judgment, and opportunity for them to express things on their mind whether it is school related, friendship or relationship related, work related, etc. will help them process their feelings. Then engaging in healthy discussions about events that have transpired in their lives further adds to their emotional knowledge.

In the moment teaching or "teachable moments" are the best times to explain emotions and feelings. When your child experiences an emotional event, talk about the experience with your child. Discuss what caused the emotion and how the event made them feel. Talk about positive and negative responses to the emotional event. For example, you might say, "You are really excited about that puppy," or "You feel frustrated with this puzzle right now."

What happened with my son is a prime example of a "teachable moment" about emotions. It was up to me as a parent to recognize the "teachable moment" and utilize the opportunity to the best of my ability. When talking with my son about how it made him feel when everyone was praising the little boy, we talked about his reaction of walking away. We discussed how walking away was not the best response to how he was feeling and that he could not always be the center of attention. There will be plenty of opportunities for "teachable moments" in your child's life to instruct him or her about emotions, but you must seize them.

Step 3

Once your child has an understanding of emotions, allow him/her the opportunity to express emotions and feelings without shame or guilt. This is especially true for older children. As I stated earlier, children need to feel they will not be judged for expressing how they feel. Learning to understand and manage feelings and emotions is a social and emotional developmental milestone. Encourage children to express feelings appropriately instead of suppressing them or expressing them without regard for others. For example, when a child is angry and acts out by hitting friends or siblings, provide an alternative way for the child to express anger such as walking away or squeezing a ball. It is important to teach children that feelings of anger and frustration are normal emotions, but they need to control how they express those emotions.

I am glad my son did not do anything mean or hurtful to the little boy such as stick out his tongue at him or not play with him anymore. I am glad he chose to walk away instead. He was able to express his feelings of jealousy in an appropriate manner. I did not make him feel guilty about how his feelings of jealousy. I assured him it was okay to feel the way he was feeling and reassured him that everyone was proud of him too.

Step 4

Children learn about feelings and emotions not only through their own experiences, but also through observing others as they encounter an emotional event. It is important the adults and role models (e.g. older siblings, cousins, friends, etc.) in your child's life, exhibit self-control when expressing their emotions and feelings. Children model the behaviors and attitudes they see others display. If we as parents and role models respond inappropriately to situations by raising our voices, cursing others out, punching a wall, sulking, etc. then we are teaching our children it is okay to respond the same way. When children see the adults in their lives displaying appropriate responses and behaviors to situations, they are more apt to adopt those behaviors. Look for teaching opportunities to show your children how to express strong feelings and emotions in appropriate ways.

Step 5

Mediate tense emotional conflicts involving children without trying to control the situation. Encourage and allow children to communicate their feelings and emotions to both peers and adults. Give your children opportunities to interact with peers and to work through social conflicts involving sharing and taking turns. This is especially beneficial with siblings where sharing and taking turns is not always present.

When conflict arises, ask a child how he or she feels and why he or she feels this way. When you get the response, ask your child what he or she thinks will help the situation. Then, encourage your child to communicate possible solutions to whoever he or she is having conflict. Assist your child in the conversation until his or her feelings have been effectively communicated to the other person and appropriate action has taken place to worked through and resolve the issue. By engaging in constructive dialogue with your child, your child will have the tools needed to handle social situations when you aren't around to mediate.

The situation between my son and the other little boy could have resulted in another ending. By talking through how my son felt during this incident, I showed him how he could handle the situation if it arises again.

Step 6

Give children the space needed to explore their feelings. If a child needs time to calm down, give him or her a soothing object (e.g. toy, book, stuffed animal, blanket, etc.) and find him or her a quiet place to be alone. Be careful not to associate quiet time with punishment or time out. Your child needs to understand needing space to experience and work through feelings and emotions is natural and not a consequence of wrong behavior.

Had my son started acting out, then I would have removed him from the situation and given him a moment to calm down and talk through what had just happened. By removing my son from the situation and discussing the events of what took place, I would have given him the space to express his emotions without condemnation. We would have been able to work through how he was feeling and label what he was feeling. However, my son chose to remove himself from the situation. Nonetheless, I was able to follow up with him regarding how he was feeling.

I hope these steps are beneficial when discussing emotions and feelings with your child. These are just some suggestions and they do not need to be followed in any particular order. Children and their behavior are unpredictable. They do not always follow a pattern or routine; therefore, as parents, we must be flexible when it comes to dealing with our children's emotions and feelings. We must be cognizant of those "teachable moments" and seize opportunities to teach our children about their emotions and feelings, the emotions and feelings or others, and how to respond appropriately to their and others' emotions and situations that arise in their lives.

Chapter 4: Investing in Emotional Health: Part 2 Hidden Needs

With the recent news coverage concerning mass school shootings by teenagers and a rise in teenage suicides, there needs to be a conversation around the emotional/mental health of our children. Children of today are faced with more challenges that previous generations. With the advent of technology and social media, children are having to contend with cyber bullying in addition to the face to face bullying that takes place at school. Bullying causes children and teenagers who cannot handle the constant ridicule and emotional abuse to develop negative self- images, lower self-esteem, depression, anxiety, and a host of other psychological problems. Children and teens who are unequipped to handle the stress associated with bullying may engage in behaviors such as becoming reclusive, running away from home, intentionally harming themselves or even worse, committing suicide.

As parents, it is our responsibility to ensure the emotional needs of our children are met so that they are able to handle the stresses of school, social media, and simply being a child or teenager in more positive ways. According to eqi.org, there are ten emotional needs of children that need to be met in order for increased psychological adjustment and maturity into adulthood. Psychological adjustment refers to how well one is able to cope with conflicting challenges and how well one is able to meet their needs in the face of difficulties or obstacles. For example, a psychologically adjusted adult might take some time off to grief the loss of a loved one whereas an adult who is not well psychologically adjusted might resort to alcohol or drugs to medicate the pain of losing a loved one or even worse, contemplate suicide. It is important children possess the skills needed to effectively deal with the pressures and challenges of life.

If ONE of these needs is not met as a child, it can lead to serious emotional and psychological adjustment as children enter adulthood. Lingering unmet emotional needs lead to improper ways of coping, constant search for something or someone to feel the emotional void in one's life, making choices contradictory to a positive, productive life.

Based on psychological research, the following pie chart provides the top eight emotional needs of children. This list is not meant to be exhaustive. It is meant to be a guide to help parents understand the emotional needs children have. Protecting our children also means protecting and cultivating the emotional needs of children so that they have a better chance at later psychological adjustment. Notice all needs are of equal importance and each need makes up the whole pie. Or in other words, the whole person. Let's look at each need in greater detail.

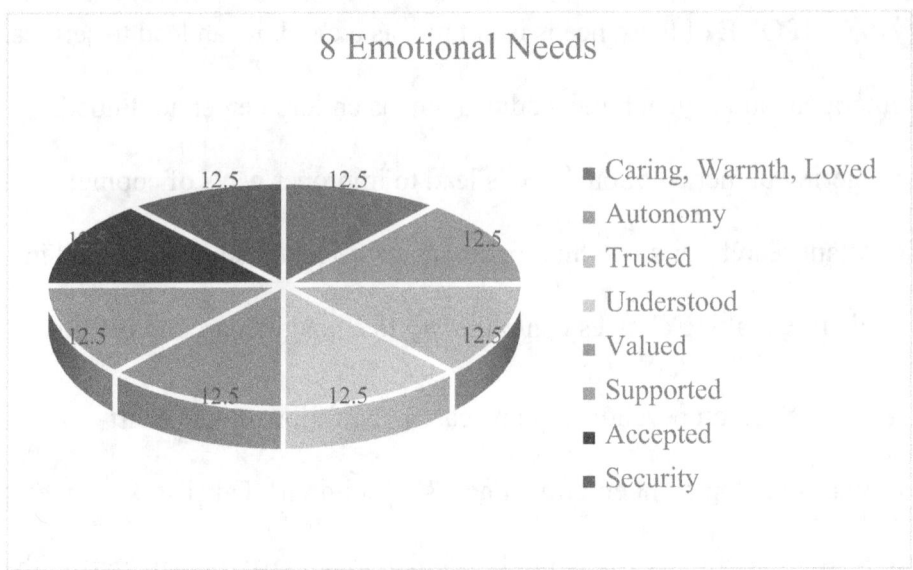

1. **Acceptance**

One day, a father and his son went to the playground to practice hitting a baseball. The father had been taking his son every weekend for the last three months to practice hitting the ball. The dad, an avid baseball player and fan, was teaching his five-year old son how to hit the baseball correctly with the bat. At some point during the practice session, the conversation went like this.

"Dad, I keep missing the ball. I can't do this. I'm ready to go"

"Son, just keep tryin'. You can do it. Just try harder. Keep your eye on the ball and swing when I tell you to."

(sullenly) "I'm doin' that. I just wanna go home. I wanna ride my bike"

(angrily) "We are not leaving until you hit the ball at least three times. Focus! You can do it."

"Get ready. Here comes the ball. Swing."

"See, dad. I missed again. I wanna…"

(angrily) "Son, we ain't leavin'. Try harder. You are going to learn how to hit a baseball. My son will know how to hit a baseball. Now, keep your eyes on the ball and swing when I say 'swing!"

"But dad…"

"No buts, son. Pay attention and swing whey I say 'swing.'"

In this illustration, we see how something so small as a father-son weekend baseball practice session can produce feelings of inadequacy, incompetence, and rejection in children. The father, in trying to improve his son's baseball abilities, can be creating a feeling of incompetence. Although the father did not come out and tell the son he was a failure for not being able to hit the baseball, his persistence at his son being able to hit a baseball lets his son know he was disappointing his father by not being able to do so. The constant practice of hitting the ball, despite the fact the son did not want to continue, is an example of how our actions as parents can trigger feelings of not being enough or inadequate. Feelings of inadequacy (not being good enough) can lead to the son feeling rejected by his father. Feelings of rejection by a parental figure may encourage children to seek acceptance elsewhere, including friends, classmates, teammates, gaming partners, other adults, etc. Each of these potential outlets of approval and recognition can have a positive or negative influence on the sense of acceptance a child feels.

Acceptance is defined as being received by a group as adequate or suitable. When children feel accepted by their parents, they feel a sense of comfort. The pressure is removed from them to perform, be, or live up to their parents' expectations. Children are at ease to simply be themselves. Investing in our children's emotional health means, as parents, we accept our children for who they are, what they can or cannot do, who they become, and how they maneuver in the world. It is not fair to ask our children to be anyone other than who they are and it is not fair to ration our love and affection based on who we think they should be. However, I want to be clear about what acceptance means. Let's not confuse acceptance with agreement. Parents may not like or agree with the decisions their children make or the adult they become, or the paths of life they choose, but they still can accept their children for who they are and love them unconditionally anyway. Parents should respect the fact their children have a mind of their own and parents should give their children the right and power to exercise their own mind free of parental control and manipulation.

Acceptance comes in many forms. Just think about all the areas in our lives that we as adults strive to be accepted. We want to be accepted by our family. We want to be accepted in our careers. We want to be accepted by our friends. We want to be accepted by our church. The list can go on and on. What I have just listed are examples of social acceptance. Social acceptance is just as important as parental acceptance. Social acceptance is being liked, positively regarded or approved of by peers, a group, organization, team, etc. Social acceptance depends upon many factors: how socially skilled an individual is, how friendly a person is perceived to be, how responsible a person is, and personal attractiveness. These are just a few factors. Notice that I did not mention sharing the same values and belief systems as a factor in social acceptance. Sharing the same belief systems and values as another person or group does not always translate into social acceptance. Social acceptance is not always based on common values. People, especially children, do not feel the need to have shared beliefs with each other in order to be accepted. Therefore, an atheist can be socially accepted by a Buddhist, Hinduist, or Christian or someone who consumes meat can be accepted by a vegetarian or someone who enjoys a plant-based diet.

As children age and mature, social acceptance becomes even more important, especially during adolescence. During adolescence, teenagers and pre-teens work hard to achieve acceptance by their peers.

Teens may choose to engage in risky behaviors or behaviors contrary to their beliefs in order to feel accepted by their peers or to fit into a desired social group. It is crucial parents promote messages of self-acceptance and help their children understand they do not need to change who they are to conform to a group or to get someone to like them.

It is important to note that we should not equate acceptance with popularity. Popularity is dependent upon how well a person's values and behavior conform to the values and behaviors of a larger group. For example, in a school where athletics is highly valued, those students who excel in sports may be perceived as the popular students. On the other hand, a school that places high value on academics will tend to view the popular students as the smarter students. We do not want to teach our children to strive to be the most popular person in their class as popularity does not equal social acceptance. We should strive to teach our children to be themselves, to accept who they are. This leads to my next type of acceptance, self-acceptance.

Self-acceptance involves taking a realistic, subjective look at one's strengths and weaknesses and concluding that you are of worth and value despite your weaknesses and flaws. Self-acceptance does not happen over-night and can take years to achieve. Self-acceptance is not automatic. It takes intentionality and subjectivity to examine the good and bad parts about ourselves. As parents, we can help our children achieve self-acceptance by first accepting them, then teaching how to accept themselves. I have listed some steps you can take as parents, teachers, coaches, counselors, etc. to assist in encouraging self-acceptance in your children.

1. Avoid allowing your children to rate themselves
2. Encourage your child to think about what they are grateful for about him/herself
3. Teach and show children the lessons learned from the good and bad experiences
4. Teach children how to forgive themselves for mistakes or bad experiences

2. Caring, Warmth, and Loved

Earlier, I talked about how parenting styles can affect the outcome of children. I discussed the four types of parenting styles and provided information on each of them. Out of the four parenting styles, the authoritative and permissive provide warm, caring home environments. However, it was only in the authoritative parenting style where the warm and caring environment was mixed with some discipline and self-control. The permissive parenting style does not provide the discipline, structure, boundaries or restraints children need to be successful and productive citizens of society.

In warm, caring, and loving environments filled with unconditional love, acceptance, encouragement, laughter, hugs and kisses, pats on the back, high fives, children feel psychologically safe to explore and try new things without the penalty of judgment, condemnation, and rejection. Warm, caring, and loving environments provide an atmosphere where children feel comfortable enough to discuss difficult or important issues without the fear of shame or disapproval from their parents. It really is true the best things in life are free: hugs, kisses, laugher, fun, and smiles. When freely given, hugs, kisses, and other affectionate touches have powerful emotional, psychological, and physical benefits for our children. Here are some interesting facts about hugs and the power of touch.

1) 8 hugs a day increases mental stability, lowers blood pressure, and reduces the risk of heart disease while 12 hugs a day improves a person's psychological development
2) An average hug is around 10 seconds long.
3) A hug benefits both parties, the one who is hugging and the one who is being hugged because of the reciprocal nature of touch.
4) Studies show children who get less hugs, learn to walk and speak late.
5) A hug a day can improve any relationship (ex: parent-child, spouse, friends, etc.) by reducing the feeling of insecurity and strengthening trust.
6) Hugs release endorphins, a hormone in the body that reduces tension and stress, boost oxytocin levels (hormone that influences social interaction), which decreases feelings of loneliness and anger, a hormone that fluences social interaction,

and release dopamine, a chemical in the body known as the pleasure hormone.[10]

On the other hand, the cold, harsh environment of an authoritarian parent can inhibit children from self-acceptance and the freedom to express themselves. Generally, these households are not full of hugs and kisses. Love and affection are not displayed. The little emotional support coupled with the limited freedom to make decisions present in an authoritarian household can cause children to become anxious, withdrawn, and unhappy, become hostile or quickly give up when frustrated. These are not traits we should not want our children to develop. Investing in our children means providing a warm, caring, and loving environment that allows them to grow and flourish without fear and shame.

Loving our children is not simply making sure they are clothed and fed every day. Loving our children extends beyond meeting their physical needs and ensuring their psychological and emotional needs are met as well. For some parents, it may be difficult to show affection to children if they did not grow up in a household where love and affection were displayed. However, we cannot allow our upbringing to determine how we rear our children or hamper us from doing things that can benefit our children. It is imperative parents not only tap into the physical needs of their children, but the emotional and psychological needs as well. By reviewing the above facts on hugs, we see how important a simple act of hugging is one brain development and functioning. Just imagine the impact of a simple hug on the emotional and psychological development of children.

3. **Autonomy**

Autonomy is defined as the ability for one to make his/her own decisions without pressure or coercion from others. Autonomy allows children to have some sense of control over decisions that affect their lives. Autonomy is NOT allowing a child to do what they want, when they want, and how they want. Autonomy is providing children with a sense of control and the ability to freely explore their interests with the implementation of boundaries to keep children safe from harm or danger. Autonomy is NOT placing the decision making of paramount decisions in the hands of children. For example, children should not be given the option of whether or not to go to school or whether or not to dress warmly when it is 20 degrees outside. Autonomy could be exercised in the ability to allow children to determine which warm outfit to wear outside.

In psychology, the concept of autonomy is an unconscious psychological need that we all have and is dependent upon one's environment to thrive. In other words, autonomy is an underlying need we all consciously or unconsciously desire and the environment we are in feeds or starves the need for autonomy. What is the environment, you ask? In the context of this discussion, the environment is the home life and psychological and emotional atmosphere established by parents. In the person-environment dialectic (child-home atmosphere), the environment can satisfy or frustrate the need for autonomy desired by children. To meet the psychological need of autonomy, parents can provide choices that are informative to their children. Informative choices are those where parents provide options for children as well as important information regarding the choices provided such as the consequences or rewards associated with their actions. In addition, parents who value autonomy ask their children about their interests so they can provide choices based on their interests. Taking note of your child's interests and incorporating their interests into the decision-making process encourages autonomy in children's lives.

For example, a parent may ask their children what they want to take to school for lunch instead of preparing it without getting their input. A parent may ask their children how they want to celebrate their birthdays rather than taking the initiative and planning something without their input. Or parents may allow their children to pick out their own clothes to wear to school instead of selecting the outfits for them. These seemingly small acts may appear insignificant, but they play a major role in establishing and promoting autonomy in children. No one, including our children, wants to be told what to do ALL the time. Even as adults, we enjoy the opportunity to make our own choices. Children are no different. Investing in our children means allowing them the opportunities to make their own informed decisions and providing choices that represent their values and interests. When parents, teachers, coaches, or others who work with children elect to use an either/or approach (ex: either do this or do that) to providing choices, we are still using some element of control, which minimizes the need of autonomy children can experience.

Providing autonomy begins early in a child's life and assists in the development of life skills. In Erickson's stages of psychological development, toddlers are faced with overcoming shame and doubt as they are allowed to explore their environment. When parents allow their toddlers to explore their environment by crawling, climbing, and walking, parents are providing their children with a sense of autonomy. The freedom toddlers experience to explore their environment provides them a feeling of autonomy. This small sense of autonomy allows toddlers the benefit of being able to make their own decisions without always needing to get affirmation from parents. When toddlers are restricted from exploring their environments, they learn to be dependent upon their caregivers for affirmation regarding what to do or not do. Toddlers can also develop a sense of fear or shame to try new and challenging things or doubt their abilities to do so. Furthermore, restricting autonomy inhibits the idea of self-sufficiency, the notion of being able to take care of one's needs. When investing in our children, we want to ensure we are developing children who can be self-sufficient, not ones who are always dependent upon others.

4. Safety/Security: Being Safe vs. Feeling Safe

Is being safe and feeling safe the same thing? Is there a difference? Let's talk about it. Pause from reading for a minute and think about this question. To you, what does it mean to be safe? When you are safe, you are free from harm or danger. The harm or danger can be physical, mental, emotional, or psychological, social, economic, spiritual, or sexual. For a long time, people have equated safety to the presence or absence of physical or emotional abuse or neglect only. However, current research shows that psychological safety is just as important as physical and emotional safety. Psychological safety involves caring for the well-being of others by providing an environment that meets the psychological needs of an individual. Psychological needs include the essentials individuals require to be well functioning adults. The eight emotional needs listed in this section are examples of some of the psychological needs children require to be well functioning adults and contribute to their overall sense of psychological safety.

Now, pause again and ponder this question. What does feeling safe mean to you? There is a difference between being safe and feeling safe. When you feel safe, you do not anticipate or expect something or someone to harm you or cause danger to you. On the flip side, when you do not feel safe, you experience emotions such as being anxiety and fear. Here's an example to illustrate my point. When you are in your house with the doors and windows closed and locked and your security system is armed, you and your family are safe from the elements of the weather (snow, rain, heat, cold), thieves and robbers, and intruders. This is deemed as being safe. However, if you have just watched a news story about an axe murder lurking the streets of your neighborhood, you may not feel as safe in your home even though you have taken the necessary precautions to keep yourself and your family safe. Fear, worry, and trepidation are present despite the fact you are safe inside your home. So, although you are safe in your home, you do not feel safe in your home.

The way we parent our children plays an important role in the safety and security our children feel. Let's go back again to the different parenting styles. The authoritative parenting style through its open communication, supportive, and flexible nature creates a comfortable, secure environment where children feel safe to share and express their thoughts, ideas, passions, dreams, and goals with their parents. On the contrary, an authoritative parenting style creates a rigid environment based on strict obedience. In this type of environment, children may not feel as psychologically safe to share their thoughts, ideas, passions, dreams, and goals for fear of embarrassment, unacceptance, punishment, or put downs from their parents. In other words, the way we talk to and treat our children during the early years of their lives will dictate how psychologically safe and secure they feel about telling us important things as they get older. Investing in our children means proving home environments and parent-child relationships that allow our children to feel safe and secure enough to shared their thoughts and feelings without fear of embarrassment, rejection, or punishment.

When my son was about three years old, he was your typical toddler getting into everything and testing his limits. One day, I was cleaning his room and found he had marked on the walls inside of his closet. I was upset and immediately went to question him about it. However, I paused before I went downstairs to "let him have it." I had to stop and think about my approach. If I went to him huffing and puffing and demanding the truth, he may or may not tell me the truth for fear of the consequences. I always talked to him about telling the truth regardless of what you think may happen if the truth is not pleasant to tell. But If I went to him with a calmer demeanor, he may feel more comfortable or safe to tell the truth.

So, I paused. Gathered my composure. Then, I gently asked him about the markings on the wall. He looked at me. Hung his head down and confessed to drawing on the wall. He immediately started to cry, knowing he was in trouble. I looked at him. Told him do not ever write on the walls again and that he was not in trouble for telling the truth. He looked relieved to not be in trouble but also a little confused. I told him as long as he always told the truth, I would not be upset with him. In that moment, I was setting the stage for how comfortable or psychologically safe my son would feel sharing good and bad things with me. The tone and demeanor we have with our children play essential roles in how psychologically safe and secure our children feel. So, although parents may provide the essentials for their children to be safe (i.e.. clothing, food, shelter), parents should also consider creating an environment and parent-child relationship through their tone and demeanor that makes their children feel safe and secure enough to share their lives with their parents.

The same principle holds true for when students are in the classroom or part of a youth group or team sport. Most children participate in group activities when they feel psychologically safe enough to do so. They engage in more discussion, volunteer more, and contribute more when they feel their actions, viewpoints, suggestions, and ideas will not jeopardize the way others view or treat them. Classrooms, youth activities, and sports should provide an inviting and welcoming atmosphere where children and youth are not afraid to be themselves and not a judgmental atmosphere that hinders children and youth from freely expressing themselves. We create welcoming environments when we choose to display a calm, rational demeanor in the tone in which we speak and the manner in which we behave.

5. Supported

When children feel safe and secure enough to share their lives with their parents, it is then up to parents to support their ideas, dreams, and goals. Will there be ideas, goals, and dreams that you will not approve or like? Will there be goals that seem lofty or outrageous? Will there be ideas, goals, and dreams you do not agree with? The answer to these questions is YES. Our children have minds, goals, dreams, and ideas all their own? Although they may be miniature versions of ourselves, they are still their own person. That's why it is important to support what they want to do or who they want to be, not what we want them to do or who we want them to be. Sometimes, in an act of control, parents will withhold resources when their children are not doing what we want them to do. This is a form of manipulation and control. Here's a real-life example of this principle.

I had a co-worker who had a son who was getting ready to graduate high school in a few months. She told me she had saved $15,000 for her son to use after he graduated. In her mind, her son was going to use the money for college. She told her son about the money she had for him when he graduated (but not the amount) and he was excited to know he was getting money after he graduated. Two months prior to graduation, my co-worker's son told her he did not want to go to college. Instead, he wanted a career in the arts. He wanted to be an actor. Now, her son always loved acting in plays at school and in the local theater, but my co-worker did not know he loved it to the extent to make it his livelihood. My co-worker was devasted at her son's news and told him a career in acting is a far-fetched dream. She told him he needed to go to college and get an education. Her son was disappointed, but thought he could persuade his mom before graduation about his decision to be an actor.

Well, graduation came and went and my co-worker's son asked to have his $15,000. He wanted to start taking acting classes at a workshop in Atlanta. My co-worker said she was not giving her son any money towards a pipe dream in acting and that if he wanted the money, he needed to enroll in a college. My co-worker made it clear to her son any money given to him would be given towards a four-year college. The son was adamant about not wanting to go to college and my co-worker was adamant about not giving her son any money towards an acting career. Needless to say, the son never got the money and begin working a 9-5 job and my co-worker ended up using the money to pay off bills. This caused tension between my co-worker and her son and put a strain on their relationship.

Just imagine how the son must have felt knowing his mother did not believe in him, his talents, his abilities, his dreams. Just imagine the disappointment in knowing your parents do not support what you want to do. Just imagine the resentment that may come later in life in knowing your parents could have helped you achieve your goals, but refused to. Just imagine! These are just a few emotions children experience when their parents do not support what they want to do. Support is not always financial. Support can be in the form of encouraging words. Support can be helping your children make the right connections with people. Support can be making sure your children have the tools they need to succeed. Support can be signing up for private lessons to hone their skills. Support takes on many forms!

Supporting our children should not be used as a means to control our children. As parents, we should not leverage our support according to what our children want to do or become. Now, I am not suggesting that we support bad behavior and illegal things, but we should allow our children the opportunity to make mistakes and learn on their own. It is our job to support and encourage them and to be there for them if things do not turn out as they had planned. Don't get me wrong. I am not suggesting that we support our children blindly. It is our responsibility as parents to gather the information needed so that we can give our support to our children when needed. Our support of our children should not be grounded in dictatorship and based on how we feel about the choices and decisions they make. Our support should be grounded in love and a desire to see our children be successful at what they choose in life. That is making a good investment in our children!

6. Trusted

Once upon a time, there was a teenaged boy who lived unhappily with this mother and step-father. He was straight A student, well mannered, and liked by most people. He was respectable and had a bright future ahead of him academically. Like most other teenaged boys, he liked to have fun on the weekends and hang out with his friends. Like some parents, his mother and step-father were a little over protective and thought they had to know his every move. When he went out to hang with his friends on the weekend, he had to tell his mother and step father exactly where he was going, who he was going with, who would be at the place he was going, what they would be doing once he got there, and how long he would be out.

To make sure he was telling the truth, his mother and step father would track his mileage on his car, which they bought for him. They would check the speedometer before he left the house and once again when he got back home. If the mileage did not add up to where he said he was, he got in trouble. The tracking of his mileage began when he started driving and even continued once he entered college. By the end of his second semester in college, he had had enough of his mother and step-father questioning his every move and tracking his mileage. He felt hostage by them because of the car and was not going to go another year living as such. In the end, the boy ended up dropping out of school, moving to another state, engaging in questionable behavior, working as a customer service representative for a small company, and buying his own car. Don't get me wrong. There is nothing wrong with being in customer service; however, the boy had the potential to be a doctor, lawyer, or CEO of a company. Soon after, the relationship with his mother and step-father quickly deteriorated and he only communicated with them once every few months.

The sad part about this story is that this boy had great potential, but his mother and step-father's lack of trust and faith in him and his ability to tell the truth made him resentful. He hated going home on college breaks and always talked about how he did not like his step-father and could not wait to move away. How do I know so much about this story? Because it happened to a classmate I knew.

Children, especially when they become teenagers, want to believe their parents trust them. Increasing their responsibilities at home, keeping open and honest communication, being consistent in your behavior as well as expecting them to be consistent in theirs, and being patient as they make mistakes are ways parents can build trust in their children. Explaining to your children about how trust is earned helps them to better understand how trust works. Children must be taught how their behavior builds or destroys trust and that once trust is lost, it is hard, often long road, to gain it back. As parents, we must teach our children that it only takes one bad act to ruin trust; however, children must also know that their parents are able to forgive them when they make mistakes and that they can regain your trust.

Often times, children engage in behaviors that cause parents to lose their trust in their children. Behaviors such as lying, stealing, cheating on test, missing curfew, or getting in trouble at school can lead to parents not trusting their children. However, there are instances where children are not displaying any questionable behavior to doubt their parent's trust. Yet, their parents still have a lack of trust. As in the case of my classmate, he was (for the most part) a good kid. He made good grades, made good choices, and did not get into any trouble, yet, his mother and step father felt they needed to keep a track of his every move. Their lack of trust in him caused him to resent them and contributed to my classmate acting out.

7. **Understood**

"You just don't understand!" How many times have you heard your child utter these words? Maybe you remember saying these words to your own parents. I remember saying these words to my parents quite often. As a teenager, I thought my parents had no clue about what I was experiencing. I thought they could not relate to what I was going through at school, with my friends, or with what it was like to be a teenager. Looking back, my parents understood what I was going through. Even though they did not grow up in the era I did, they still experienced peer pressure and some of the same issues I was going through. There is a saying that goes "There is nothing new under the sun." Issues such as peer pressure and bullying have existed for decades, just on different levels.

Understanding your child begins with seeking information such as what are their interests/hobbies, what do they like or don't like, what do they enjoy doing, what music, food, clothing, etc. do they like or do not like, or what makes them happy or sad. Understanding your children begins by having a desire or interest in being a part of their world, not simply tolerating or ignoring their likes and dislikes. Information seeking (in other words asking probing questions) is easier completed when the lines of communication are kept open between parents and children. Noticing and observing subtle changes in your child's behavior, interests, friends, habits, speech, style of dress, music selection can provide insight into your children.

One of the best ways to gather information about your child is during meal time. Dinner time is a great time to ask questions about how your child's day was at school, how your child's day was at practice, or how their day was with their friends. Having discussions around the dinner table provides a less threatening and more welcoming environment for children to express themselves. In these moments, it is not your job as a parent to scold, chastise, and discipline. Rather it is your time to listen to what's on your child's heart and gain insight into what's important to them. It's time to connect with your children in a welcoming atmosphere.

Car rides are another opportunity that parents can take advantage of to connect with their children. A car ride free of distractions such as the radio, music, or cell phone is an optimal time for parents and children to have and enjoy meaningful discussions. As my son gets older, I am finding that we have some of our best conversations during the car ride home from daycare. He appears more open to discussing his day at school then rather than waiting to get home and I use that time to affirm him if he's had a rough day. Again, my purpose at this point is not to scold and chastise him, but to gain insight inside how he feels and what he thinks. You may find that other times of the day work better for you to connect and better understand your child. That is perfectly okay. These are not the only times you can utilize to connect with your children. The key is finding the times that work best for you and your child. Remember, when children feel understood, they experience a feeling of being loved, appreciated, accepted, and valued, which leads me to the last important emotion children need to experience, being valued.

8. Valued/Validated

Do you know how you got your last name? Last names became popular around 1,000 years ago. Back then, the world was smaller than what it is now. People did not travel too far from their home and it was common to only use one name (what we call today first names) to identify people. As the population increased, people started to travel more throughout the world, and the number of people with the same first name increased, it became necessary to identify people using another name.

Beginning in the 16th century, people began to identify themselves according to their occupation or talent, what they looked like, or geographic location. So, Michael who is a baker became Michael, the baker and later Michael Baker. And Michael who likes to hunt became Michael, the hunter and later Michael Hunter. Or Mary who had brown hair would become Mary Brown and Mary who lived on a hill became Mary Hill. The purpose of this distinction was not so much to establish last names, but to ensure people knew which person was the topic of discussion. However, distinctives were not passed down from father to son; therefore, you could have Michael Baker who had a son named Robert Smith (aka, the blacksmith). Centuries later, these distinctions soon evolved into standard last names, beginning within the family unit first. Therefore, children began taking on the father's last name.

Why do I share this piece of history with you? I wanted you to see how last names added value to a person. No longer were people identified by their first name only. People were recognized by what they did, they occupation, or where they lived, adding value to an individual and validating their existence. Our children are no different from those who lived centuries ago. They desire to be valued and validated according to who they are and what they do. When something or someone has value, it means the object or the person is worth something. And when something or someone has value or is valuable to you, you treat it or the person differently.

Our children want to know they, their opinions, their feelings, their ideas and dreams, their existence matters to us. Children want to know when they talk with their parents, their parents are actually listening and taking their feelings, opinions, and ideas into consideration when making decisions or choosing a course of action. When we value our children, we treat them with respect and dignity. We do not purposely embarrass them or make them feel bad or treat them as if they do not matter to us. It pains me when I hear a news report about parenting abusing, neglecting, or mistreating their children. Abuse and neglect can be physical or emotional as in the way we treat and talk to our children. Protecting our greatest investment means ensuring we value our children and making them feel as if they are of value.

To validate means to confirm or approve something or someone. When we validate something or someone, we are simply saying "I appreciate you." "I hear you." "I see you." In simple terms, validation is recognition. Recognizing one's accomplishments, worth, value, feelings and emotions, behaviors, and talents and interests. Validation begins at home first between parent and child. Children look to their parents to validate who they are. When your kindergartener brings home a drawing and you have no clue what it is, you still smile and say "You did a good job." Even though you have no clue what it is, you still acknowledge your kindergarten's efforts. I do not know of any parent who would tell their kindergarten a picture they drew was "ugly" or tell their kindergartener "You cannot draw. I can't tell what it is." Shame on a mother or father who does that!

As children get older, they desire and need validation more. If they do not receive validation at home, they will seek it elsewhere. They will seek it from friends, teachers, coaches, boyfriends/girlfriends, or anybody who will validate them. It is imperative parents recognize and celebrate the uniqueness their children possess. This can be accomplished by offering words of appreciation for the things your children do or say, commenting on your child's interests, talents, and strengths, supporting their ideas and dreams, and acknowledging their feelings and emotions.

Chapter 5: Educational Health: Mindsets, Goals, and Education

How involved we are as parents in our children's education and our parenting styles and practices play a critical role in socializing and orienting children towards academic success. When parents engage in behaviors such as academic monitoring and academic support, they are contributing to their child's overall educational health. Academic support involves the extent to which parents encourage, assist, and support their children's academic behaviors and outcomes. By academic behaviors and outcomes, I am referring to test grades, study habits, graduating from high school, entrance into college, completion of projects, attending school regularly. Helping with homework, reading with your child, assisting them in studying for a test, and supporting their children's academic choices are examples of academic support. On the other hand, academic monitoring entails the behavioral constraints parents use to control academic behaviors and outcomes. Behavioral constraints include monitoring the amount of study versus play time and reviewing progress on assignments and test grades periodically.[11]

Much research exists showing how parental involvement, parenting practices, and parenting styles affect the emotional/psychological well-being and academic outcomes of children. Research supports the notion emotional health and well-being is essential for good academic success. When children have negative emotions such as anger, anxiety, or sadness, their grades tend to decrease. One reason for the decrease in grades is the presence of negative emotions tend to decrease a child's motivation to learn and engage in classroom or school activities. All of a sudden, an A student can turn into a C student based on their emotions and how they are handling their emotions. The same effect is true for children who display positive emotions such as joy and pride. Students with positive emotions tend to participate more in classroom activities, engage in appropriate classroom behavior, show more interest in learning, put forth more effort to learn, and obtain better grades.[12]

Educational outcomes are also impacted by parental style and parenting practices. Children are more motivated to succeed when their parents are actively engaged in their learning. Engagement can be instilling positive beliefs and attitudes about their children's abilities and the importance of education and/or academic monitoring and support. For parents, it is imperative we teach and show our children about the value and importance of education. Research shows as children internalize their parents' beliefs and values about education and their abilities, they are likely to be intrinsically motivated to learn, more motivated to engage in behaviors, and exert effort that contributes to their academic goals.[11]

In addition, parental views on the concepts of ability and effort help shape the expectations placed on a child and how the child internalizes the concept of effort and ability affects his/her achievement motivation and educational outcomes. Ability refers to the capabilities or competencies of our children, understanding what they can and cannot do. Effort refers to the amount of time and energy spent to complete a task. In other words, parents who view their child as competent and capable and value the effort exerted when it comes to studying for tests and getting good grades will often yield children who possess similar views about their own abilities and effort exerted. Children will put forth more effort and believe in their abilities more when their parents value effort and see their children as capable and competent.[11]

Fixed Mindset Vs. Growth Mindset

In better understanding how we as parents view ability and effort, let's examine the concepts of a fixed mindset and a growth mindset as they relate to our children and their abilities. The belief that individuals have abilities and qualities that are set or fixed, meaning those abilities and qualities are permanent and not changing regardless of what effort is exerted to change them is a belief in a fixed mindset. Parents who believe their children's abilities and qualities (e.g. intelligence, personality, talents) are fixed think their children either possess the ability to do something or they don't. They are either smart or not smart, an extrovert or introvert, creative or not creative and so on by nature. When parents adopt a fixed mindset regarding their children's abilities, the amount of effort the child puts forth has little to do with how much their ability to do or not do something will increase or decrease.

For example, a parent may view a child's ability in math as fixed if the child consistently performs below average in math despite how much the child studies. As a result, the parent will consciously or unconsciously expect the child to perform poorly in math, resulting in low expectations of their child to perform well in math. The fixed mindset can be applied when a child possesses a high ability to do something as well. For example, if your child is very creative, then as a parent you will consciously or unconsciously expect your child to do well in subjects such as art or music despite the effort your child puts forth in class by the sheer nature your child is creative. Simply stated, parents who adopt a fixed mindset view their children's abilities as absolute and set expectations about their performance accordingly.

On the other hand, the belief that our abilities and qualities are malleable and capable to change depending on the amount of effort exerted is a growth mindset. Parents who view their child's abilities, talents, and skills with a growth mindset believe their child's qualities are capable of increasing or improving when effort is put forth. In other words, a person's abilities can grow, increase, and strengthen according to the amount of effort, practice, or training applied. Parents with a growth mindset regarding their children's abilities thinks "the more their children try and the more their children learn, the better they get." Therefore, their child has the capability to become better, smarter, stronger, at what he/she does according to the amount of effort, training, and practice their child exudes. As a result, parents who adopt a grow mindset regarding their children's abilities tend to have higher expectations of their children's performance in school. They believe their child's current abilities can grow to the extent of the effort made in the process.

Research shows when children adopt a growth mindset over a fixed mindset about their abilities, they tend to perform better in school because they view their abilities as capable of improving. Therefore, they are more willing to put forth effort in studying and paying attention in class to increase their educational performance. Parents play a critical role in our children view themselves. Investing in our children means helping them adopt a growth mindset regarding their abilities and attributes so they are more motivated to put forth their best efforts in school. If children view their abilities as qualities that will not change regardless of the amount of effort made, they may not be as motivated to do their best in school due to low expectations of change.

If you are wondering how to foster a growth mindset in your children, I have an answer for you. When children receive praise based upon their abilities, they tend to adopt a fixed mindset. For example, if your child receives an "A" on an assignment and your praise sounds something like this "Good job. You are really good at _____" or "You are a smart boy/girl.," you are praising their ability; therefore, they are more prone to accept the belief their intelligence is fixed. On the other hand, if your child receives a "A" on an assignment and your praise sounds something like this "I can see you worked hard on this" or "Good job. You did your best.," then you are praising their efforts, not ability, and your child is more apt to adopt a growth mindset regarding their intelligence. Similarly, criticizing your child's ability or effort with statements such as "You can do better than that." "I am disappointed in you." "Think of another way to do it." can produce the same type of results, except this time, they may view their intelligence or ability as low.

As parents, we must be cognizant of what we say to our children. Our words are shaping the way our children view themselves. I employ you encourage your children to work hard and put forth an effort to do well in school, assuring them their efforts to improve are not in vain. Refrain from too much or constant criticism and focus on the efforts made. If you are a parent and you believe qualities and abilities in your children are fixed, I challenge you to be open to the idea that your children's abilities and qualities have the potential to change. Focus on the efforts made to improve and not your child's inabilities.

Goal Setting and Goal Striving

Goal setting and goal striving are other factors that contribute to our children's educational success. Many people set goals, but not everyone attains the goals that are set. It is not enough to just have goals without a definitive course of action to achieve the goals. To achieve goals, we must demonstrate goal striving. Goal striving is the effort, persistence, attention, and planning one puts into accomplishing a goal. It is a mental map of the actions we are going to take to accomplish our goals and it keeps us on the right track to achieving our goals. Having goals and a clear action plan (goal striving) to accomplish goals help to enhance performance and increase attainment of goals. Both goal setting AND goal striving are essential to attaining goals.

Research shows simply having goals leads to goal-directed behavior. Goal directed behavior are the actions one takes to accomplish a goal. Goal directed behaviors could be setting aside time each day to work on a goal, saving a specific amount of money each month, exercising regularly, staying on a budget, eliminating fast food from your diet, practicing a hobby or sport for a specified amount of time each day, and so forth. Whatever you do to achieve a goal is goal directed behavior and we tend to engage in these behaviors more when we have a goal we are striving to accomplish. When we are not working towards a goal, we can waste valuable time, money, effort, and energy on things that do not matter or become idle, lazy, and stagnant doing nothing at all.

How does this translate into education? Let's take a look. Much of our children's academic success is related to his/her ability to set, strive for, and attain educational goals. Educational goals vary depending on each child's needs, strengths, weakness, effort, support, competencies, and desired end result. Educational goals can include passing a test, making a good grade on an assignment or project, scoring well on tests such as the ACT or SAT, etc. The goal is what your child views as important. If the goal is important to them, they will put forth more effort and be more persistent in attaining their goals. It is our responsibility as parents, teachers, coaches, pastors, counselors, etc. to assist children in setting goals and devising an action plan to achieve those goals. When we do this, we are investing in our children.

Secondly, the difficulty of the goal dictates the amount of effort a child will put towards the goal to accomplish it. If a goal is too easy, a child will put forth minimal effort to achieve it; however, a goal that is more difficult will require a child to put forth more effort to achieve it and promotes persistence. Therefore, it is critical children learn how to set difficult, yet attainable goals to maximize their efforts AND how to strive for their goals. This is not just true in regards to education. Setting and striving for difficult, but attainable goals can be applied across many disciplines, interests, and areas (health, finances, career, etc.) of a child's life. Accomplishing goals requires effective goal setting and goal striving. Let's look at the steps in goal setting and goal striving.

1. **Identifying the objective to be accomplished** – (ex: making all As, passing a test, increasing your GPA, saving money, losing weight, etc.) The objective simply states what you wish to

accomplish. Setting the goal(s) is how you plan to accomplish the objective.

2.   **Defining the difficulty of the goal** – A goal should have a level of difficulty that is attainable, but also requires one to put forth effort and persistence in achieving it. Therefore, the goal should not be too easy where it is accomplished with little or no effort. On the other hand, it should not be too difficult where striving for the goal becomes frustrating, causing you to want to give up.

3.   **Clarifying the specifics of the goal** – A goal should be clearly defined so that one knows exactly what to do. Simply telling someone to "do your best" or "study hard" does not clearly define what the expectation is. Phrasing goals using this language does not provide a target and are left open to different people's interpretation. "Do your best" could mean making a "C" for one person or making an "A" for another person. A more specific goal would be to read one chapter a day or make at least a "B" on a test. Using more specific language allows provides you with a clearer understanding of the expectation.

4.   **Specifying how and when performance will be measured**. – Goals should state how one will evaluate progress towards a goal and when progress will be assessed.

Setting goals is only half of what it takes to accomplish a goal. As parents, we should assist our children in striving for their goals. Goal striving is the second part of reaching our goals. Often times, we simply set goals but do not state how we will strive to attain the goal. Goal striving is just as important as setting the goal. Goal striving provides you with an action plan to accomplish your goal. The next steps in accomplishing goals is the goal striving portion.

5. **Identifying strategies to accomplish a goal** – It is essential children and parents decide on the steps or action plan necessary to accomplish a goal and refining the action plan into one that has the potential to accomplish a goal. (ex: Strategies for passing a test could be to review notes from school, re-read certain content areas, study with a partner, etc.)

6. **Creating "if-then" implementation intentions** – "If-then" statements help children anticipate situations that may occur that lead to them accomplishing their goal or not ("if" part) and provides them with a response to a situation ("then" part). For example, if the goal is for a child to make an "A" on a test, studying for the test is essential. If a friend asks him/her to go to the movies instead of studying, the child must make an appropriate response to the request.

Already anticipating situations such as these as well as the appropriate response will help children stay on task and continue to strive for their goal.

7. **Providing continuous feedback** – To accomplish a goal, having continuous feedback provides children with a sense of how they are doing in attaining a goal. Feedback can be how well a child is doing when quizzed on information that will be on a test or completing the PSAT as a gauge to how well one will perform on the SAT. Feedback is the litmus test for how well our children are accomplishing their goals

Children set, strive for, and attain educational goals according to their and their parent's expectations, attitudes, and beliefs about education, ability, and effort. Setting high academic expectations for your children demonstrates to them education is a valued belief. When parents communicate and reinforce educational beliefs and attitudes, these beliefs are then internalized by their children, thus providing the motivation children need to succeed. Investing in our children means investing in their education and instilling in them values and beliefs that promote learning and educational success.

Chapter 6: Investing in Relational Health: Navigating Relationships

"No man is an island entire of itself; every man
is a piece of the continent, a part of the main;" John Donne

Children in today's society are exposed to so much more technology than children growing up just thirty years ago. When you look back just thirty years ago, cell phones were not found in the hands of everyone. Computers were not commonplace devices in the home. The internet and social media did not permeate every aspects of our lives. With technology comes the ability to connect more with people in different cities, states, countries, and continents. Technology allows us access to information whenever and wherever we need it. For these reasons, one could argue technology has had a positive effect on how we operate our daily lives.

Technology has also altered the way we interact with each other. We can send a quick text message or direct message (DM) to those connected to us. We can send an email to co-workers. We can post information, announcements, flyers, etc. send invitations, and share photos of celebrations, vacations, and good times with family and friends on our social media pages. Long gone are the days of writing and mailing invitations for birthday, anniversary, or retirement parties. We can do all these things without ever having to directly talk to someone on the phone or face to face. For this reason, one could argue technology has made society lazy and disrupted the way in which humans interact with each other.

As a result, the art of conversation and dialogue has become a lost, antiquated art form. People use text messages and emails as means of communicating important information that should be discussed in person or at least during a conversation on the phone. Some people are ending relationships over text messages or social media posts. Some people are having in depth conversations about critical issues via text messages and DMs. The problem with using these platforms to communicate is that it can be difficult to accurately convey one's emotion, intent, or feelings without hearing the tone in which someone is saying something. The reader has to infer intent when reading an email, text message, or DM. And sometimes, the wrong intent is implied, which can lead to communication breakdowns, arguments, and fights. Another issue with using digital formats to communicate is that people can be less sensitive. It is easier to send a nasty email or text message to someone than to say the same horrible things to a person's face. People can hide behind digital formats and say things they may not necessarily say in person. I believe this is one reason why bullying, especially on social media, is so prevalent in our schools.

Investing in our children means equipping them with the skills needed to effectively communicate with others as well as equipping them with the ability to establish and maintain positive personal and professional relationships. The relationships our children have with others can positively or negatively impact their lives. Just think about the saying, "Birds of a feather flock together." The platonic, romantic, and professional relationships our children choose greatly influences the trajectory of their lives. Therefore, we must provide our children with the tools and information needed to foster, cultivate, manage, and sustain healthy relationships.

Most of us possess the psychological need of relatedness, the sense of belonging to or communing with someone or a group. Relatedness is an underlying need similar to the psychological need of autonomy. Whether we realize it or not, most of us have an innate desire to commune with others. I would venture to say most people enjoy going to the movies with someone, having a nice meal with someone special, going to a football game with friends, shopping with a best friend, or hanging out with friends or family at home. The same is true of children. I would venture to say most children have an innate need to be liked and have someone to play with on the playground at school or have someone to sit beside and eat lunch with in the cafeteria. As with most things, there are exceptions to the rule. There are some people who appear to be content being by themselves; however, I believe, we were made to fellowship with one another and not live life as a hermit.

I believe it is most parents' desire for their children to succeed in life. Although how one defines success is up for debate, wanting success or to be successful is something most people desire. Whether it is success at relationships, in a career, at home, at school, at church, in sports, or at a hobby, the purpose of engaging in these activities is to achieve some level of success. Success could be as simple as making the football team or being the star quarterback, graduating from high school or obtaining a doctorate degree, or playing in a local band or playing before millions of cheering fans. How a person defines success determines the measures one takes to achieve a certain level of success. As parents, it is our responsibility to lay the foundation for our children to be successful and that foundation begins in the home.

During the nine months a baby is growing inside his mother's womb, he or she is not consciously concerned about receiving proper nutrition, being left alone, maintaining a constant body temperature or other essentials for life. These items are provided for in the safety of the mother's womb and through the umbilical cord that attaches the baby to the mother. However, once outside the womb and the umbilical cord is cut, the baby enters a new world, a new environment where he or she becomes dependent on another to meet the basic nutritional, clothing, emotional and safety needs that were once met unconsciously in the womb. Now, the baby looks towards the mother or the primary caregiver to meet those needs. Therefore, the first bond formed out of the womb is the mother-child relationship or the primary caregiver-child relationship. This relationship sets the tone for future connections, friendships, and relationships the child will form later in life.

One of the first goals of an infant is to establish a sense of trust of the new environment, the one outside the womb and with those in the new environment such as mothers, fathers, siblings, nurses, etc. If you can, try to imagine how a little infant must feel as he senses the force of his mother's push moving him out of a warm, safe habitat into an unknown, cold environment. He or she is leaving the safety of a familiar environment where all needs are met and involuntarily entering a world that he/she must now figure out how to get his or her needs met. He or she must now trust the outside world to provide what the inside world was providing. No wonder an infant comes out of the womb crying! I would too.

Trust is generally established with the person who feeds, bathes, and interacts with the infant the most. Typically, this person is the mother or a maternal figure such as a grandmother, aunt, sibling, etc. However, it can be other relatives or caregivers. As the infant's physical and emotional needs are met on a consistent basis, trust develops between the infant and the caregiver. If needs are met inconsistently by the caregiver (typically the mother), the infant can develop frustration and discomfort instead of pleasure and enjoyment from the interactions. The interactions of frustration and discomfort can lead to a sense of mistrust of the world for the infant. This sense of mistrust can persist throughout the child's life and as they enter adulthood, making attempts to develop relationships and form bonds with other people more difficult.

Being able to effectively relate with others is an innate need in people. Establishing and managing relationships is crucial to one's psychological well-being. We were not created to go through and experience life by ourselves. As the saying at the beginning of the chapter says, "no man is an island entire of himself." Whether we want to admit it or not, we are connected to one another. We need peer relationships, parent-child relationships, employer-employee relationships, sibling relationships, business relationships, etc. in order to maintain a state of well-being and to be successful. There is not one successful person who can say they were successful all on their own, without the aid of others. It is impossible because we were created to be interdependent, not independent. Interdependence is not being dependent on others, but it is realizing that you need others to succeed.

Successful people need great team members, great partners, and mentors to help them achieve their goals. You cannot achieve success on your own. Personal and business relationships are crucial to one's success. It is crucial to the success of your children.

As children age, peer relationships, both platonic and romantic, become much more important factor in pre-teen and teenagers' lives. The desire to be liked by someone or to fit in a group or clique is greater as compared to elementary age. It is also during adolescence where peer relationships have a greater influence on a child's words, thoughts, and actions when compared to parental relationships. During adolescence, children are trying to figure out who they are, what they believe, and how they fit into society. They rely more on input from their peers than from their parents; therefore, it is critical strong parental-child relationships are established early in life. Good parent-child relationships that feature open communication, honesty and trust, and autonomy can help children navigate peer relationships as the get older.

Investing in our children means providing them with the tools necessary to navigate different relationships in their lives. One tool necessary for navigating relationships is the ability to identify positive or healthy versus negative or unhealthy friendships and relationships. It is essential as parents that we first possess positive, healthy relationships in our lives so that we are able to model what healthy positive, interactions should look like. It can be difficult to teach our children what a positive relationship or friendship resembles when we, as parents, do not have a positive or healthy relationship in our lives. Remember, parents are a child's first teachers and what a parent models at home greatly influences how a child thinks, what he or she says, and what he or she does.

So, what are traits of a positive, healthy relationship we should model for our children or at the very least teach them about? The table below provides a list of traits associated with positive, healthy relationships and traits of negative, unhealthy relationships. These are not the only traits that compromise a positive, healthy relationship or friendship. It is just a list of some of the traits. Relationships that contain even one negative, unhealthy trait should be ended as soon as possible. Review this list with your children and teach them the traits of both positive and negative relationships so they are able to recognize when they are in a healthy vs. unhealthy relationship.

Traits of a Positive, Healthy Relationship	Traits of a Negative, Unhealthy Relationship
Mutual Respect – each person feels valued and each other's boundaries are understood	**Disrespect** – making fun of your friend or partner's interests, hobbies, feelings, or opinions
Trust – give person the benefit of the doubt	**Hostility** – antagonizes the other person or picks fights
Honesty – build trust and strengthens relationships and friendships	**Dishonesty** – lying or withholding information from your partner or friend
Compromise – each person is willing to give and take, everything is not one person's way	**Control** – one person makes all the decision regarding the relationship, isolates the other from family and friends, unreasonably jealous
Individuality – identity is not based on the other person and individuality is not compromised for the sake of the relationship	**Dependence** – feeling as if you cannot live without the other person, making threats if the relationship ends
Good Communication – speak honestly and openly about issues and feelings without fear or shame	**Intimidation** – one person exercises control by making the other feel fearful or timid
Anger Control – dealing with anger by taking deep breaths,	**Abuse (Physical, Mental, Emotional, Verbal and/or**

counting to 10, or stepping away from a situation	**Sexual)** – acts of violence such as punching, slapping, kicking, etc., words of degradation such as insults and name calling, forcing oneself upon another without consent
Fighting Fair – stick to the subject and avoid the use of insults	
Conflict Resolution – being able to identify problems rationally and calmly and talking through solutions rather than yelling and screaming or making threats	
Understanding – taking time to understand how others feel	

Once you have taught your child about healthy vs unhealthy relationships and friendships, the next step is allowing them to engage in friendships and relationships, intervening when necessary to discourage or end a negative or unhealthy relationship. Keeping an open line of communication and asking your child questions about his or her friendships and relationships is one way to stay involved in who they are interacting with on a regular basis. Also, monitoring their social media accounts and supervising play dates and outings are other methods of staying abreast as to who your child is associating with outside of your presence. Going through your child's social media accounts and cell phone may feel like an invasion of privacy, but as minors, children have limited privacy rights, especially when you are the one taking care of their needs. If we are going to invest in our children, we need to invest helping them navigate the friendships and relationships (business or personal) in their lives.

Chapter 7: Investing in Financial Health: Money Matters

The adage "If I knew then, what I know now, I…" has never been truer when it comes to financial literacy and success. There are some lessons we learn as we experience life and then there are some lessons we learn from the experience of others. One of my favorite quotes from my pastor is "If you do not heed the instructions of others, pain will be your teacher." So many times, I have found that saying to be true, especially when it comes to finances.

Ever since I had my first job as a daycare worker, I have been good at saving and managing money. Although, I was good at saving and managing money, I was not financially literate. I was not well versed in investing, retirement planning, the stock market, bonds, and mutual funds, FICO scores and credit reports, or any other financial matters. I knew enough to get life insurance while I was young so that I would have a lower monthly premium and I knew it was important to have a good credit score, but I did not understand how my credit score affected my interest rate and monthly payment or how my financial habits affected my credit score. Beyond the saving and managing money, having good credit, and obtaining life insurance, I was financially ignorant. At the time, I did not know how financially illiterate I was. It was not until later in my thirties that I realized how much I did not know about finances. And the lessons I did learn, came through painful experiences and life circumstances. Had I been under the tutelage of someone with financial knowledge, I would be further along in my finances.

Part of protecting your investment in your children is equipping them with the tools necessary for good financial health and literacy. Financial literacy prepares them to be able to effectively manage money and resources in order to function in a society where money is essential to having a decent quality of life. I have mentioned the term financial literacy. Now, let's define what it is. Financial literacy is defined as "the ability to use knowledge and skills to manage financial resources effectively for a lifetime of financial well-being." I like this definition of financial literacy because it talks about a "lifetime of financial well-being." Financial literacy is more than just knowing how to earn money and spend money. More importantly, financial literacy is knowing how to manage money (earning, spending, and saving money). Money can be easy to obtain, but difficult to manage. Just ask the numerous celebrities who have made millions, but who are broke and/or destitute now.

According to recent studies, less than 60% of Americans would pass a 30-question financial literacy test that covered topics such as budgeting, paying bills, interest, and other financial topics. That means there are many people in America who do not understand the ins and outs of financial matters. Let's test your financial literacy before we start. Here are seven true/false statements. Answer these statements to the best of your knowledge. Do not peak ahead. I have provided answers and explanations along with the sources of the answers and explanations for you to review.

Statements:

1. The price of bonds lowers as interest rates rise. True/False

2. A loan costs you more when calculated using simple interest versus compounding interest. True/False

3. APR (annual percentage rate) is the same thing as interest rate. True/False

4. With a Roth IRA (individual retirement account), you will have to pay taxes on the money you withdraw at retirement age. True/False

5. There are three major credit reporting agencies. True/False

6. "Dow Jones" or "The Dow" and Nasdaq report how well stocks are performing in the stock market. True/False

7. The length of your credit history (e.g. 5 year credit history vs. 15 year credit history) is the most important factor that affects your credit score. True/False

Answers:

1. The price of bonds lowers as interest rates rise. **True** - According to Forbes.com, as interest rates rise, the value of existing bonds go down.

2. A loan costs you more when calculated using simple interest versus compounding interest. **False** - Simple interest paid or received over a certain period is a fixed percentage of the principal amount that was borrowed or lent. For example, a person obtains a simple interest loan for $18,000 with an annual

interest rate of 6% that is to be repaid over three years. The amount of simple interest paid over three years will be $18,000 (loan amount) x 0.06 (interest rate) x 3 (period of the loan) = $3240. The total amount repaid on the loan will be $18,000 (original loan amount) + $3,240 (simple interest) = $21,240.

Compound interest is interest on interest. It is calculated by multiplying the principal amount by the annual interest rate raised to the number of compound periods. Compound interest accrues on the principal amount and the accumulated interest of previous periods. For example, if the person in the above example obtained a compound interest loan for $18,000. The amount of compound interest to be paid will be $18,000 x $((1.06)^3 - 1)$ = $3,438.29. Therefore, the total amount repaid on the loan will be $18,000 + $3438.29 = $21,438.29.
http://www.investopedia.com

3. APR (annual percentage rate) is the same thing as interest rate. **False** - The interest rate is the cost of borrowing the principal loan amount. It can be variable or fixed, but it's always expressed as a percentage. The APR is a broader measure of the cost of your mortgage because it reflects the interest rate, as well as other costs such as broker fees, discount points and some closing costs. The APR is also expressed as a percentage.
http://www.bankrate.com/finance

4. With a Roth IRA (individual retirement account), you will have to pay taxes on the money you withdraw at retirement age. **False** – You will not pay taxes when you withdraw your contributions, and you will not pay federal taxes on your earnings, as long as the five-year aging requirement has been met. With a traditional IRA, you will pay taxes when you withdraw your pre-tax contributions and when you withdraw any earnings.
https://www.fidelity.com/retirement-ira

5. There are three major credit reporting agencies. **True** – According to https://www.usa.gov/credit-reports, the three major credit reporting agencies are Equifax, Transunion, and Experian.

6. "Dow Jones" or "The Dow" and Nasdaq report how well stocks are performing in the stock market. **True -** Both the Dow Jones Industrial Average (DJIA) and the Nasdaq (National Association of Securities Dealers Automated Quotations) exchange refer to an index, or an average of a bunch of numbers derived from the price movements of certain stocks. The DJIA tracks the performance of 30 different companies that are considered major players in their industries. The Nasdaq Composite, on the other hand, tracks approximately 4,000 stocks, all of which are traded on the Nasdaq exchange. The DJIA is composed mainly of companies found on the NYSE (New York Stock Exchange), with only a couple of Nasdaq-listed stocks such as Apple (AAPL), Intel (INTC), Cisco (CSCO), and Microsoft (MSFT). http://www.investopedia.com

7. The length of your credit history (e.g. 5 year credit history vs. 15 year credit history) is the most important factor that affects your credit score. **False** – Payment history is the most important factor that contributes to your credit score. Creditors want to ensure you are someone who pays debts on time and not someone who pays late before extending you more credit. Lenders are more prone to lend money to those who have a good history of paying their debts on time.

A close second important factor is debt amount at 30%. Lenders want to know how much debt you currently owe before lending you more money. The higher your debt amount (i.e. auto loans, student loans, mortgage, credit cards, etc.) is in relation to your income the more likely a lender may be hesitant to lend you more money. Therefore, it is beneficial to keep your debt amount low.

Below is a diagram that represents the factors that affect your credit score and what percentage they affect your credit score.

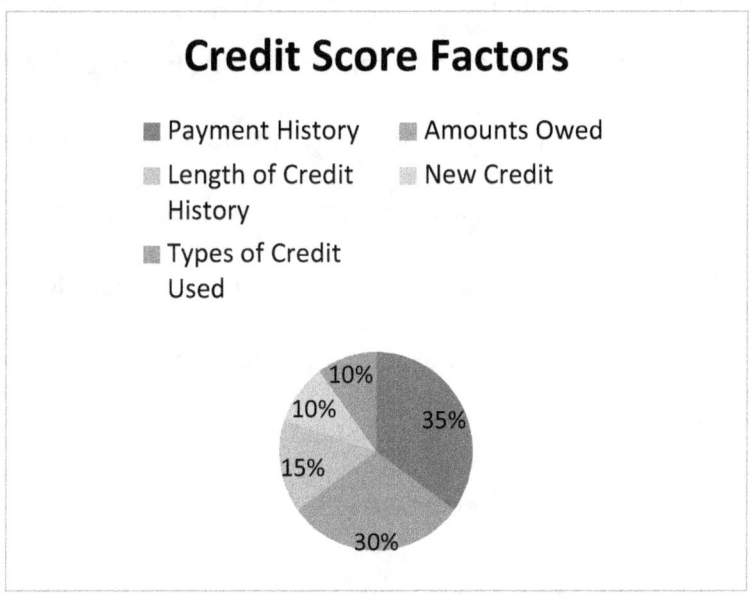

http://www.investopedia.com/articles/pf/10/credit-score-factors.asp

Finances is one of those topics that unless you know a lot about it, most people shy away from it. Money is something we all need, but it is also a subject some people are uncomfortable discussing. Many of the lessons I have learned about finances did not come from my parents, but from reading books and magazines, talking with people who had financial success, and meeting with a financial advisor. My parents were not knowledgeable about finances; therefore, they were unable to share pearls of wisdom with me regarding my finances. They did share what little they knew, which was saving money. However, they did not discuss investing with me. As I began the journey of better finances, I began to understand that good financial health was more than just saving money. Good financial health and wealth require investing money. Saving money will not always make you wealthy, but investing money in the right places can. Once I began to learn the nuances of finances, the more intrigued I was at learning more. And the more I learned about finances, the more I realized my financial health was poor. Regardless of what financial situation I was in at the time, I knew I possessed the power to change it if I was willing to take a different perspective on my finances. That was encouraging for me.

Why is financial literacy important?
1. Saving Habits - From birth to age 21, children are exposed to approximately 1 million advertisements. These advertisements condition children early on to consume products whether it be toys, clothing, electronics, food, etc.
2. Budgeting Skills – helps you reach financial goals and targets
3. Financial Independence/Freedom – the ability to buy what you need without having to consult your bank account
4. Better Decision Making – allows one to make more informed decisions about money
5. Debt Reduction – knowing how to avoid and/or eliminate debt

Investing in our children's financial health means providing them with the information and resources needed to effectively manage their finances. It does not mean providing children with everything they want without providing them with the understanding of what it takes to have the means to get whatever you want. As parents, it is our responsible to teach children the value of a dollar and to remind them of the saying "Money does not grow on trees." Children are not born with an innate sense of money matters. It is up to parents to teach money management so that children can avoid the pitfalls of bankruptcy, foreclosures, high credit card debt, and other financial burdens. It is our job to teach them about the consequences of debt, the importance of having good credit, and saving and investing for the future.

Often times, parents are guilty of making sure a child has his or her every want and desire without teaching them basic money management. Children acquire possessions without understanding the value of money and how to earn it to survive. In some of these instances, when children reach adulthood, they are still financially dependent on their parents for basic necessities (food, clothing, and shelter) because they have not learned how to take care of themselves by earning a living and living within their means. Budgeting money is a life skill that, when learned early in life, will enable children to more successfully transition into adulthood with fewer financial hurdles to overcome. Teaching children about money matters prepares them to be financially independent adults and to be able to make informed decisions regarding the use of their money (e.g. mortgages, loans, investing, achieving financial goals, etc.).

Children as young as three years old have some basic knowledge about money. Children watch as their parents enter a store or business and use money to obtain various goods and services. From this simple act, children learn early on that money is a tool used to get items and services you want and need. However, nowadays, with the rampant use of credit and debit cards, children can develop an unrealistic sense of money. As they watch their parents, swipe and insert plastic cards in a machine, children may not fully understand or appreciate how it takes money (dollars and coins) to purchase items. It is not as simple as swiping a card to get what you want. The plastic card still has money attached to it and is unusable without money. Making a conscious effort to use dollars and coins instead of debit and credit cards at stores can be helpful in children understanding and appreciating the value of money. Children as young as preschool age can start to learn about different coins and paper bills and their respective values. Simple activities such as counting coins and paper bills to make different value (e.g. 50 cents, 30 cents, $2. 50, $7.00, etc.) and showing children what $1.00 can buy vs. $10.00 are ways parents can begin to teach young children about money and its worth, and what it can buy.

After teaching children about what money is, it is important to share with them how money is earned. Again, children see their parents get money from their wallet or purse or from the bank or an ATM machine; however, they still may not fully grasp how money is earned. This is an opportunity for parents to talk to their children about how they earn money from their job or career. Explaining to children how we work (i.e. use our skills and knowledge) to earn money is key in understanding how money is earned rather than freely given to us. Furthermore, discussing how different skill and knowledge levels equate to different amounts of money earned helps children better grasp how the skills and knowledge they learn can affect the amount of money they earn later in life. Then, parents can talk about entrepreneurship and starting and owning your own business.

Earning an allowance is a great way for children to learn about the importance of earning money and money management. In some instances, children are required to perform chores around the house such as cleaning their rooms, washing dishes, mopping and sweeping the floors, or taking out the trash in exchange for a monetary gift. In other cases, children may not be required to do household chores. Instead, they may earn money based on achieving certain grades in school. More importantly than how children earn their allowance is the money management lesson that follows the allowance. After you hand your child his/her allowance is a prime opportunity to teach them about investing or saving some of their money instead of spending all of it. Putting limits on how allowance is given helps children better understand finances too. Parents should hold firm to the amount of allowance they give their children and not give any more money when their children have spent all of their money. This simple act, which may not sound so simple when your child is begging you for more money, teaches children about managing what is given to them.

When children receive birthday and Christmas money, this is another opportunity for parents to teach children about saving and investing money. Instead of allowing your child to spend all of the money they receive, show them how to spend a portion of it and save the rest. The amount or percentage saved is not as important as the lesson of saving. Parents can also open a bank account for their children to put their money in or show them how to save up for a big purchase. Many banking institutions offer student accounts (anyone under a certain age) with no minimum balance requirements and/or monthly fees. These accounts are great for young children and teenagers to help them develop a sense of money matters. Opening a back account gives children practice in reading a monthly bank statement or viewing it online, understanding a simplified concept of interest, teaches them concepts such as deposits and withdrawals, and helps them see how their money is growing or decreasing in their account. Research financial institutions in your area and see which ones offer student accounts or something similar.

Parents can also allow their children to suffer the natural consequences of their financial choices. This is another method of helping children gain a better understanding of how money functions. For example, if they damage their car, let them pay for the repairs instead of you paying for the repairs. Here is another example. Give your child the responsibility of paying for their school lunch, school supplies and extra-curricular activities out of the allowance you give them. What is left can be spent of fun stuff. This act teaches children to be responsible for the necessities of life and not to spend money on frivolous purchases. In order for children to learn the lesson, we as parents have to provide opportunities for them to use their knowledge and skills. The earlier parents start with teaching their children about money, the more time children will have to learn, understand, and apply their knowledge about money. It is an important lesson on the difference between wants and needs. It is crucial we teach our children the importance of distinguishing a want from a need to ensure needs are met first and then wants in regards to money management. Food, clothing, transportation, utilities are examples of needs whereas electronics, entertainment, and toys are examples of wants. Looking through magazines and books or browsing in stores and determining what items are a need and which ones are a want is one way to help young children make the distinction between wants and needs.

In addition, when money is earned versus given to a person, money if often times perceived as being more valuable because you worked for it. As people, we have a tendency to place more value on things we work for than those things that are simply given to us. For example, we often appreciate our first car more when we have worked for it versus if it was given to us as a birthday or graduation present. Thus, we tend to take care better care of the car because we know the effort and time it took to earn enough money to purchase the car. We do not want to see our time and effort squandered away.

Additionally, it is important children earn money or an allowance instead of merely giving money or an allowance without any work or effort required. Earning money helps to alleviate the pitfall of entitlement and creates good work habits and ethics. Entitlement suggests one has a right to gain something (e.g. money, privileges, clothes, electronics, etc.) without putting forth any effort in obtaining it. This is not a message we should want to send our children. Good work ethics and habits consist of self-discipline and self-control to complete tasks in the allotted time, being responsible for your actions and their consequences, and appreciating the value of hard work. Investing in our children means preparing them to be financial independent so they are able to take care of themselves and instilling good work habits and ethics in them so they are able to maintain a job or career.

Once children comprehend how money is earned, it is necessary children learn to make good spending choices with their money. Now, that you have discussed the difference between wants and needs, children need to learn how to spend their money wisely, even if it is on something they want. In order for children to learn money management, it is important children recognize why they want or are buying a particular item. Having children make a list of reasons to buy an item and reasons not to buy an item is one way to help them make better spending choices. The goal is to get children to ponder the pros and cons of their purchases in order to make more informed spending choices, especially if they are using some or all of their money towards a purchase. Nonetheless, the ultimate decision to make a purchase should be left to the child to decide.

Another concept in money management is being able to save for short-term financial goals. When young children put money into a piggy bank, they are developing a rudimentary concept of saving. Through this simple concept, children are beginning to learn that money is saved towards a future purchase. Saving money can be short term as in saving up to purchase a new video game or long term as in saving up to purchase a car or have money for college. Teaching children about short term vs. long term money goals also helps when it comes to spending and managing money. Delayed gratification is a concept that even some adults still grapple with today. It is our human nature to want what we want when we want it; however, in terms of money management, there will be times when we have to put our current desires and wants on hold until we have the money to purchase them. Learning the concept of delayed gratification early in life helps with money management later in life.

Assisting your child in establishing a written system of money earned and money saved towards a goal can help your child stay focused and motivated to continue with the goal. In this regard, children can see their effort and progress towards a goal. It is vital parents do not step in and give their child the money needed towards a goal as this act can undermine their child's effort and progress, decrease the sense of accomplishment children feel in saving money, and create the idea that parents will always be there to bail out their children during financial hardships. Again, the goal should be for our children to be self-sufficient.

Many people do not have the distinction of graduating with a degree in finance or economics. Therefore, they have to rely on the knowledge and expertise of those who have earned a degree or those who have experienced financial success. Do not allow the excuse that you may not be good with money to prevent you from teaching your children about finances. If you do not know much about finances, do not be afraid to learn from those who do. Go to a seminar or read books on money management. There is a plethora of knowledge just waiting to be unearthed. When it comes to financial literacy, ignorance is not always bliss.

Chapter 8: Investing in Spiritual Health: Finding Their Way

Most of us have been to a business or social function mingling with people we do not know. Generally, at these functions, people engage in small talk to keep a peaceful and pleasant exchange among those in attendance. Topics may include such things as current events, family, career, or the stock market. Politics and religion are the two topics most people avoid. Religion is often a hot button topic for people to talk about. No other subject, besides politics, can incite a barrage of powerful emotions and feelings such as anger, frustration, indignation, annoyance hurt, shame, disappointment, upset, etc. The topics of politics and religion are so contentious because of how polarized they have become, especially in America. Finding a middle ground or point of compromise is hard to do because of the strong positions some people take when it comes to politics or religion. In religious and political conversations, it can be difficult for the parties involved in the conversation to simply agree to disagree. In religious or political debates, people often times adopt a "my way" is the right way philosophy. They are unwilling to listen to ideas or beliefs contrary to their own. Or they work overtime trying to get the other side to see things their way.

With the advent of technology, the world is becoming less separated and more connected globally. The world is not a collection of isolated land masses anymore. People and land are becoming more interconnected and more easily accessible. People are traveling internationally more and realizing there is more out there to see and do. People are realizing more and more that other cultures exist and everyone does not think, act, or behave the way they do. No longer are people separated by geography. Another country or culture is just a plane, boat, train ride, or mouse click away on the computer. We are not bound by physical locations anymore and you do not need to leave the United States to experience different cultures. The United States has always been a melting pot of people with different beliefs, attitudes, thoughts, and ways of doing things. We are only bound by our limited thoughts, ideas, and views. Once we are willing to open our minds to new ideas and possibilities, then we are at a place to grow.

Protecting our greatest investment, our children, also requires investing in their spiritual health and well-being. Spiritual health and well-being entails having joy, peace, fulfillment in life, and an altruistic view towards others that promote compassion, love, and forgiveness. Spiritual health and well-being provide one with a moral compass by which to make decisions in life. For example, do I seek revenge when someone has wronged me or do I forgive and let go? Do I cheat on a test by looking at someone else's answer to get a better grade or do I do the best I can on my own? Spirituality or lack thereof influences the everyday decisions we make and how we govern ourselves.

One's religious faith, beliefs, values, principles, and morals help shape and define one's sense of spirituality. Spirituality is NOT the same as religion. Spirituality differs from religion in many ways. From the research I conducted for this book, there are numerous ways to define religion and spirituality. One definition describes religion as an "organized system of beliefs, practices, and symbols designed to facilitate closeness to the transcendent, and to foster an understanding of one's relationship and responsibility to others in living together in a community." The transcendent, something or someone outside of one's self, represents God, Allah, or a Higher Power in Western religions and the "manifestations of Brahman, Buddha, Dao, or an ultimate truth/reality in Eastern religions.[13] Another definition states religion is "the belief in and worship of a superhuman controlling power, especially a personal God or gods."[13] Spirituality, on the other hand, is defined by some as a search or quest, or discovery of the transcendent that leads to a belief or nonbelief that turns into devotion.[13] or "relating to or affecting the human spirit or soul as opposed to material or physical things."

Many people confuse spirituality and religion or use these two terms interchangeably, but they are distinctively different. Let's take a look at how they differ.

Religion	Spirituality
1. Tells you what is true	1. Allows you to discover truths through your personal experiences
2. Based on following rules about conduct and rituals and adhering to punishment for not following the rules	2. Relies on the principle that there are consequences, be it good or bad, for our actions

3. Makes you dependent upon someone or something to determine what is right or wrong	3. Makes you independent, discovering what is right and wrong based on internal convictions
4. Divides the different religions	4. Unites the different religions

With that said, I am not here to promote one religion, belief, or way of thinking over another. I am not here to promote organized religion over spirituality or vice versa. I am here to help you realize and understand the benefits of investing in your child's spiritual well-being and health. The method or form (religion or spirituality) you choose to achieve this goal is completely up to you. There are numerous benefits to children having good spiritual well-being and health. Research has shown children who engage in spiritual and/or religious practices tend to display more positive emotions such as hope, altruism, compassion, optimism, happiness, gratitude, kindness, hospitality, forgiveness, and have a sense of purpose and meaning for their lives. Children, who have been intruded to some concept of religion or spirituality, also tend to know the difference between right and wrong and are better able to accept the consequences of their actions.

While engaging in simple activities at home and having discussions about religious beliefs and principles that delineate what is considered right behavior and what is considered wrong behavior, parents are making the investment in their children's spiritual health. The investment into your child's spiritual health during the younger years helps them as they enter adolescence and adulthood to cope with adversity, depression, anxiety, fear, rebellion, and other dilemmas as their experience the trials and tribulation of life. Without some sort of spiritual or religious foundation, research shows children (and adults) are more prone to respond to the pressures of life via suicide, drug or alcohol abuse, promiscuity, or other maladaptive means.

Embracing spirituality and religion is not limited to just going to and participating in church, mosque, temple, or synagogue activities. There is nothing wrong with attending functions held by organized religious institutions. But parents can perform other activities at home to promote spirituality and religious beliefs. Below are just a few examples of what parents can do at home to promote spirituality and religious beliefs and the corresponding belief(s) they can encourage. Keep in mind, both the child and the parent can benefit from engagement in these activities. Children benefit by learning principles to help them succeed in life. By watching their parents partake in these activities, children have a model and a guide to help them explore and understand various spiritual concepts and beliefs. When parents engage in these activities, their spiritual concepts and beliefs are strengthened as they demonstrate their importance and relevance to their children.

Activity	Concept/Belief
1. Giving thanks before a meal.	Gratitude
2. Saying prayers at night to a higher being	Reverence
3. Discussing daily events in a child's life using open ended questions	Enthusiasm, Forgiveness, Openness, Listening, Compassion
4. Taking nature walks	Unity, Connection
5. Talking about characters on television or in books	Empathy, Compassion, Hospitality
6. Scheduling downtown time at home (no electronics) or a moment of silence	Meditation, Reverence
7. Reading books on topics about kindness, justice, being fair, etc.	Kindness, Justice, Fairness, Etc.

Morality

There was a mother who had a gravely ill child at home. She took her child to the doctor and the doctor provided the mother with a prescription for a specific type of medicine to heal her sick child as well as a list of ten pharmacies to call. Not many pharmacies in the area carried the specific medicine the mother needed for her child. The mother began to call each local pharmacy to see who had this specific type of medicine in stock. No one had the specific medicine she needed. The mother was getting desperate and anxious because no one had the medicine she needed to save her child. Now, the mother was down to the last pharmacy on the list. She dialed the phone number, waited for pharmacist to pick up, and proceeded to ask about the medicine she needed. This was her final chance at saving her daughter's life. Tears of joy started streaming down the mother's face as she heard the words "We have what you need in stock." Overcome with joy and adulation the mother quickly hung up the phone and rushed to the pharmacy.

When she arrived at the pharmacy, the pharmacist told her the medicine was going to cost $1500.00. The mother was flabbergasted at the price the pharmacist was charging her for the medicine. The pharmacist knew the medicine the mother needed was rare and decided to charge her an exuberant amount of money for it. The mother passionately explained how she desperately needed the medicine to safe her sick child's life and begged and pleaded with the pharmacist to lower the price of the medicine. The pharmacist would not lower the price of the medicine. Dishearten, the mother left the pharmacy, got in her car, and drove home.

Knowing she had to do all she could for her sick child, the mother returned to the pharmacy later that night. She was determined to get the medicine her sick child needed. Therefore, she decided to break in the store and steal the medicine she needed. Here's the question, was the mother justified in stealing the medicine? What would you have done? These are questions that concern morality, justice, and what's fair. Depending on your point of view, belief system, morals and values, you may feel the mother was justified in stealing the medicine or you may feel stealing in wrong regardless of the circumstance. Morality is one area we as parents must help our children navigate so they are able to make better choices in life.

Morality is often associated with what is right, good, just versus what is wrong, bad, or unjust. However, it encompasses more than just what is right or wrong. Morality also involves the rights and responsibilities of not only you, but also others. Morality entails a level of decision making that governs our thoughts, words, actions and behaviors. Morality is often derived from our own personal belief system, principles, values, and concepts. And those beliefs, principles, values, and concepts are often derived from some form of spiritual and/or religious teachings, whether knowingly or unknowingly.[14]

Christians use the teachings of Christ as a moral compass to guide their decision making and actions. Muslims use the teachings of Allah as a guide. Buddhists follow the teachings of the Buddha and followers of Hinduism rely on the philosophies of their religion as a moral guide for their behavior. These are just a few examples of religions and religious teachings practiced around the world.

Parents play a vital role in the moral development of children, whether the basis for morality is grounded in spirituality and religion or not. As the saying goes, parents are a child's first teachers. It is imperative parents discuss issues such as what is considered right and wrong or acceptable and unacceptable language and behavior as well as model moral behavior and speech in front of their children. Once again, parents cannot take the attitude of "Do as I say, not as I do." Children are very observant and watch closely what those in positions of influence do and say. Our children are watching how we treat others, what we say to others, and how we say things to others. They are also taking note of the effects of our actions, words, and behaviors and how they impact others. They are learning lessons from us so we must be cognizant of what our actions, words, and behaviors are teaching them. Investing in our children means instilling in them principles, values, and a belief system that encourages them to be the best version of themselves they can be.

Bullying

It seems as if some children today are less compassionate, less empathetic, more cruel, meaner, and heartless. I am amazed at the lack of compassion children have for other children. I have seen this behavior in children as young as three years of age. Some children feel embolden to say anything or to do anything to whoever they want to without regard for other's feelings. I feel strongly that the rise of social media, the public's obsession with guns and violence via video games and movies, and the lack of parental involvement in the homes contribute to the increase and type of bullying behaviors children display. It is a sad state of affairs when children do not possess the basic personality traits to be friendly, kind, and courteous to other children. These personality traits should be nurtured and developed in children in hopes they would not engage in bullying behaviors as they get older.

Bullying has become a national epidemic in our school system. And technology and social media have not made this dire situation any easier. Did you know over 3.2 million students are bullied each year and 17% of American students report being bullied between 2-3x a month or semester? Did you also know 90% of children between 4th and 8th grade report being bullied and 1 out of 10 teens drop out of school because of repeated bullying? Children are committing suicide at an alarming rate due to obsessive and repeated bullying at school. Where has society and culture dropped the ball with bullying?[15]

The sad thing is bullying is not just something we experience in our childhood. Bullying has become more and more popular among adults. Whether it is making rude, mean, nasty, inappropriate comments, mistreatment of others, abuse of power and authority, belittling, and/or public humiliation, adults are just as guilty of bullying as children are. Social media and reality television have made it easier for our society to engage in bullying practices on a grander stage. We can watch people being bullied anywhere in the world and for some people, it is a form of entertainment to see someone tortured. As a society, we have lost our sense of compassion and empathy for humanity and someone else's pain and agony has become our pleasure and joy.

According to stopbullying.gov, bullying is defined as "unwanted, aggressive behavior among school aged children that involves a real or perceived power imbalance. The behavior is repeated, or has the potential to be repeated, over time." Bullying can be physical, emotional, verbal, or social in nature and each type can be devastating to children. Physical bullying is the act of hitting, punching, pushing, kicking, slapping, or other means of physical aggression upon someone else. It can also encompass taking other's possessions or belongings. Boys are more prone to engage in physical bullying than girls. Emotional bullying is described as causing emotional harm or pain to someone and often involves isolating or excluding an individual from others or social routines. Emotional bullying can involve the spreading of lies and rumors with the intent to humiliate someone or using language that incites fear in someone. Girls are more prone to engage in emotional bullying than boys.

Verbal bullying is the use of language that negatively impacts one's self-concept, self-image, and self-esteem via mocking, demeaning, degrading or insulting another person. Verbal bullying involves teasing, name calling, taunting, and other behaviors verbally abusive behaviors. Lastly, social bullying entails purposely isolating a child out of a game, event, or activity, embarrassing someone in public, spreading rumors about others, and encouraging others not to be friends with a child. Most often, bullying occurs at school or on the bus ride to school and home from school. Bullying can occur on the playground during recess, in a local neighborhood, or on social media outlets. Each form of bullying, whether it occurs alone or together, has lasting effects on those who are bullied.

Often times, bullying involves an imbalance of power. Children who bully may not necessarily be physically stronger than those they bully. Bullies know how to use their physical strength, embarrassing information, or words with the intention to control and/or harm those they are bullying. In the book, <u>Little Girls Can Be Mean</u>, the authors discuss how children between the ages of kindergarten and 2nd grade typically do not display intentional acts of harm towards other children. Generally, it is not until 3rd grade and beyond children began to show signs of engaging in behaviors or speech with the deliberate intent to harm others. Around 3rd grade, children began to understand how their actions and behaviors can affect others. Also, around this age, children are experimenting with how to exercise their personal power and control over their social circumstances. According to stopbullying.gov, children who bully display the following characteristics:

- Aggressiveness or easily frustrated
- Have less parental involvement at home or are having issues at home
- Think badly of others

- Have difficulty following rules
- View violence in a positive way
- Have friends who bully others

These same children are also more likely to

- Get into physical or verbal fights
- Have friends who bully others
- Increase aggressiveness
- Get sent to the principal's office or to detention frequently
- Have unexplained extra money or new belongings
- Blame others for their problems
- Not accept responsibility for their actions
- Be competitive and worry about their reputation or popularity

Therefore, as parents, it is essential we began early with instilling principles of love, compassion, empathy, forgiveness, and other positive emotions, attitudes, and behaviors in our children. Often times, these attributes are rooted in some form of religion or spiritual practices. We should not want them to grow up to bully others. When we see our children displaying the above bullying behaviors, we should correct them and use those instances as teachable moments to discuss the negative side effects of bullying. Investing in the spiritual health and well-being of our children aids them in being better friends, playmates, classmates, teammates, partners, and people as they get older.

Chapter 9: Conclusion: Final Thoughts

The song "Greatest Love of All" was first sung by George Benson in 1977 and later made popular by Whitney Houston in 1985. The song talks about how today's children are tomorrow's future and the importance of teaching and showing each individual child his or her unique beauty. The song may sound cliché when referring to children, but there is much truth to be found in these simple lyrics. As parents, we are rearing children who will be our future leaders, doctors, politicians, engineers, teachers, lawyers, mechanics, and so on. Our children are the ones who will be making decisions that will impact our future, our well-being, our health, our environment, our world. It is our responsibility as parents to equip our children with the tools necessary for them to be successful in life and to be productive citizens of society. We are to teach them so they can "lead the way" for themselves and others and not be dependent and rely on others to figure out life.

As the song lyric continues, we are to show our children "the beauty they possess inside." The beauty of their self-worth. The beauty of their abilities, talents, and strengths. The beauty of their ideas, thoughts, hopes, dreams, and goals. The beauty of their flaws, imperfections, and weaknesses. Our children are unique in their own way and it is our job to help them embrace and celebrate their uniqueness. We are not to be critical and judgmental. When parents show their children how beautiful they are on the inside and outside and that they are perfectly imperfect human beings, children develop a sense of pride about who they are. They can carry this sense of pride into the world and be an agent of change for the welfare of their environment, society, and the world.

Protecting our greatest investment, our children, is not always going to be easy. It is not always going to be fun. It is not always going to feel right. However, just like long term investments, it is essential we as parents stay the course, keep our eyes on the return of our investment (successful, well-adjusted adults), and not waver in our responsibilities as parents. From birth to age 18, we are not our children's friends. We are the authority figure, representative, and model for how to navigate life in a way that is not detrimental to their physical, emotional/educational, relational, financial, and spiritual health and well-being. We, as parents, must not take this responsibility lightly. Parents have been charged with ensuring most, if not ALL, needs of their children are met to the best of our capabilities: physical, emotional/educational, relational, financial, and spiritual. It is not enough to simply provide food, shelter, and clothing for children and neglect the other needs they have if we want them to be well-adjusted adults.

Much emphasis was placed on investing in the emotional needs of children. It is easier for most people to overcome financial, spiritual, physical, and relational deficiencies as they become adults than to overcome emotional deficiencies. In adulthood, our children can learn how to be better stewards of their money if their parents did not teach them. They can, as adults, obtain spiritual guidance if their parents did not instill in them spiritual principles. They can learn to eat healthier and lose weight if their parents did not promote healthy eating habits and exercise when they were younger. They can get educated and counseling on dealing with relationships. However, emotional deficiencies that occur in childhood can cripple socio-emotional and psychological development and well-being in adulthood and often affect the decisions and choices our children will make later in life.

Unresolved and unrepaired psycho-emotional issues can often lead to emotionally and psychologically damaged adults who have difficulty functioning in the work place or in their careers, in school, in relationships and friendships, and in life. They may suffer with trust issues, acceptance, low self-esteem, etc. due to situations that may have arose from their childhood. It is easier to simply suppress or not acknowledge emotional issues we possess as adults than to deal with our emotional baggage. That is why it is imperative as parents we do not neglect the emotional needs of our children and take the time and effort to invest in them.

After age 18, we can become our children's friend, confidant, mentor, advisor, etc. as they have transitioned from child to adult according to society's rules and standards. It is at this point, age 18, when we must trust the teachings, morals, values, and principles we have instilled in them earlier and allow them to "lead the way." Protecting our investment requires time, effort, patience, tenacity, determination, and most of all a commitment to our children to provide them with the tools and techniques necessary to be successful adults.

Will we make mistakes as parents? Will we fall short at times? Will we make the wrong decisions sometimes? Will we have regrets about the way we handled certain situations? The answers to these questions are a resounding yes, yes, yes, and yes. Parents are still human and as humans, we will make mistakes. There has never been nor will there be the perfect parent because we are not perfect people. The key is to not beat yourself up about past mistakes, regrets, and failures. Learn from the error of your ways and make it your mission to be a better, more informed, more intentional parent. It is never too late to start over. Investing in our children is not about being the perfect parent and not making mistakes. However, investing in our children is more about being cognizant of the various needs of our children AND devising ideas and actions to meet those needs. The information presented in this book is designed to arm parents with information about the needs of children and guide them as they rear their children. It is not enough for parents to read this book and take in the knowledge without having an action plan to implement the knowledge learned. There must be application of the information.

If you have gotten this far in the book, I think it is safe to say you have read the contents of the book up until now. Therefore, I would like to challenge you to meditate on the material you have read and really think about how you are parenting your children. Think about the areas you are excelling in regarding your parenting skills. Then, consider the areas in your parenting skills you can improve upon. We all have areas we can improve upon. There are no perfect parents as I mentioned before. Because there are no perfect parents, there will be no perfect children. The goal of this book is not to shame parents who may feel they are not up to par in their parenting practices. The aim of this book is not to rear perfect children to be perfect adults. The purpose of this book has been to be a guide to educate parents as well as teachers, coaches, counselors, youth pastors and other who interact with children on how to better invest in our youth in order to meet the various needs they possess. I hope you have found value in the information presented in this book and are better equipped to protect your greatest investment, our children!

Notes:

1 – Wheelwright, V. (2011). The power of the long-term perspective. Bethesada, MD: World Future Society.

2 - www.cdc.gov/healthyschools/obesity/facts.htm

3 – www.heart.org

4 - www.Sugarstack.com

5 - www.health.harvard.edu/staying-healthy/the-truth-about-fats-bad-and-good

6 -Spera, C. (2005). A review of the relationship among parenting practices, parenting styles, and adolescent school achievement. *Educational Psychology Review*, 17(2), 125-146. DOI: 10.1007/s10648-005-3950-1

7-Topor, D.V., Keane, S.P., Shelton, T.L., & Calkins, S.D. (2010). Parent involvement and student academic performance: A multiple meditational analysis. Journal of Prevention and Intervention in the Community, 38(3), 183-197. doi: 10.1080/10852352.2010.486297

8- www.parentingforbrain.com/4-baumrind-parenting-styles/

9- Reeve, J. (2015). Understanding motivation and emotion. (6th ed.). Hoboken, NJ: John Wiley and Sons.

10 – www.trendsnhealth.com

11- Kashahu, L.,Dibra, G., Osmanaga, F., & Bushati, J. (2014). The relationship between parental demographics, parenting styles and student academic achievement. European Scientific Journal, 10(13), 237-251.

12 - Valiente, C., Swanson, J., & Eisenberg, N. (2012). Linking students'emotions and academic achievement: When and why emotions matter. *Child Development Perspective*, 6(2), 129-135. doi: 10.1111/j.1750-8606.2011.00192.x

13 - Koenig, H. (2012). Religion, spirituality, and health: The research and clinical implications., ISRN Psychiatry. doi: 10.5402/2012/278730

14-Poramate Pitak-Arnnop, Kittipong Dhanuthai, Alexander Hemprich, and Niels C. Pausch (2012). Morality, ethics, norms and research misconduct. Journal of conservative dentistry 15(1). 92-93. doi: 10.4103/0972-0707.92617

15 – stopbullying.gov

ABOUT THE AUTHOR

Ashley S Jefferies, MA CCC-SLP, M Ed. has worked in the field of speech-language pathology for the past seventeen years. She received her bachelor's degree from Tennessee State University in speech pathology, her first master's degree from The University of Tennessee, Knoxville in speech pathology, and her second master's degree from The University of Alabama, Tuscaloosa in educational psychology. Mrs. Jefferies has worked in the clinic, school setting, and natural environment with children with special needs such as autism, Down syndrome, cerebral palsy and other medical conditions, helping them increase their overall speech and language abilities for improved communication skills.

She is also the owner of First Words, LLC, a pediatric therapy company that offers speech/language therapy services to children to help improve their communication skills. Ashley has conducted continuing education classes regarding speech, language, and cognitive development for child care center workers and other health care professionals. Additionally, Ashley has undergone research in increasing creativity in the classroom, the role of parent, student, and school in achieving educational outcomes, and the correlation between emotional intelligence/regulation and academic achievement.

www.ingramcontent.com/pod-product-compliance
Lightning Source LLC
LaVergne TN
LVHW051558070426
835507LV00021B/2639